Piero della Francesca and the Early Renaissance

Philip Hendy

Piero della Francesca and the Early Renaissance

The Macmillan Company   New York

Library of Congress Catalog Card Number: 68–24113

First American Edition
Originally published in Great Britain in 1968
by George Weidenfeld and Nicolson Ltd, London
Designed by Gerald Cinamon
Printed and bound in Great Britain

Contents

Preface

It is more than half a century since Roberto Longhi published a now famous article on Piero della Francesca and the evolution of Venetian painting. His thesis was among the most illuminating in the literature of painting; for the undeniable fact to which he drew attention, that it was Piero whose pictures showed Antonello da Messina and Giovanni Bellini how to see and to paint, has a significance far beyond the immediate context. It was from the school that these two founded in Venice that the subsequent European tradition put forth its several branches. Thus from the moment of Longhi's discovery that he was the link between Florence and Bruges and Venice Piero has had to be recognised not merely as the central pillar of the classic Italian Renaissance but as the living bole of this European tree which continued in leaf and flower until less than fifty years ago.

That Michelangelo may have been inspired by the figure-drawing of Luca Signorelli, the one great painter who is known to have been actually Piero's pupil, is scarcely relevant. Signorelli had strayed back into a Florentine tradition which had become more linear, and he developed only a part of his master's teaching. The world's debt to Piero is on an altogether different scale.

It was not so much because he was neither a Florentine nor a Venetian, nor even a Roman, or because his studio, though – symbolically enough – in the heart of Italy, was off the beaten track that the debt went all those years unrecognised. It was rather because of its very magnitude and diffusion. The force and manner of the great stylists have been so easy to trace in their descendants that they rouse the suspicion today of having inhibited a more liberal growth. The sheer completeness of Piero's vision, without bias, defying dissection or analysis, allowed Heinrich Wölfflin to write *Die Klassische Kunst* in 1898 without mentioning his work. The developments which it stimulated were too broad, too live to attract his academic eye. In them nature continued to be studied and vision remained integrated with design. Three centuries later, the wayward airborne figures of Tiepolo could scarcely be more different from Piero's grave men and women firmly planted on the earth; but they all inhabit the same universe of reality idealised, of space and light and air.

Piero can have ceased to be an unacknowledged influence only when all accessible 'old masters' had become equally academic under the decayed varnishes which limited the space in them and brought natural colours near to an appearance of brown monochrome. Then the 'Impressionists' had to rediscover for themselves the beauty of pure colours in sunshine, and the identity of colour with form and with light. How ironical that Piero's work should be first held up as an example to modern painters by teachers frightened of 'Impressionism'! When they subjected Seurat at the École des Beaux-Arts to the influence of dark copies from his dusty frescoes, among many others of the Italian Renaissance, it must have been for the sake of the architectonic qualities which they shared with the rest rather than for the significance of his colour, which has neither style nor date.

8   Longhi's many subsequent studies not only of Piero and his life and works but of all the literature concerning them, so very scarce in early days, so rapidly proliferating since he published his *Piero della Francesca* in 1927, are all accumulated in Volume III of his collected writings, published in 1962. In this rich quarry of material, where the almost level strata of a *catalogue raisonné* and a bibliography of more than four hundred items are interspersed with glittering but more uneven layers of free interpretation, the chronology of the stratification is left undisguised. As in nature, there is a certain confusion, which has to be reduced before the material can be fully appreciated. After the second edition, of 1947, Kenneth Clark did a public service in carving out a shapely block of manageable proportions, recognising that not everything was gold which glittered and rejecting some of the wilder veins. His beautifully written *Piero della Francesca* was published in 1951. In the year of my writing, 1967, Oreste del Buono and Pierluigi de' Vecchi have published their conscientiously exhaustive *L'Opera completa di Piero della Francesca*, with a *catalogue raisonné* and a résumé of the facts and the valid references, which incidentally bring Longhi up to date.

Piero seems to have made little use of assistants – when he painted a banner for a small confraternity at the height of his fame he seems to have done it all by himself. For this reason and because of his strength of character there is only the smallest fringe of disputable works, and it would seem pointless for me to attempt yet another catalogue. I have merely been careful to mention in the following pages every picture which I believe to be authentic. With publications like those of Longhi and De' Vecchi in print, it would be plagiarism as well as pedantry to parade once more a list of references which are of no interest to the general reader, for whom this book is principally intended. I have seasoned with as little as possible of this kind of caviar, though I have found unavoidable a few old-fashioned footnotes to express a particular indebtedness or to indicate the sources where their interpretation is unusually important or the dispute particularly hot. I have rarely given the reader warning where my interpretations of Piero's works or their chronology differ from those of my predecessors. This often happens, for the great facts about Piero della Francesca are his pictures, and, with the exception of a bare half-dozen, the sadly few documents are also capable of interpretation. If my own *Piero della Francesca* fails to convince the reader, it will be not through a deficiency of footnotes or of argument, but because no sufficiently consistent image sequence of events has been achieved.

PHILIP HENDY

7 December 1967

1. *The Nativity*, panel 124.5 × 52.5 cms. National Gallery, London

I

1 · A Picture by Piero della Francesca

In *The Nativity* by Piero della Francesca the air is so pure, the light so clear that 1-11 65* we can discern a score of miles away the outlines of what seem to be the minutest of hills become mere pimples on the curve of the earth. It is the curve alone which dictates how far we are able to see; and the pale, cloudless sky reflected in the meandering river is an even more infinite infinity, seeming to promise eternal peace.

This endless vista is at the very edge of the picture, and it would not be surprising if it distracted our attention from the rest of the scene, so close upon us, which is its subject: the Angels singing over the new-born Child the first of all Christmas hymns. Instead, it works not only by contrast to bring what is near nearer and more immediate but to establish its significance, to prove its sanctity.

The picture can only have been an altarpiece, and those who knelt below the altar saw above it, through the pilasters of the gilded frame, the Madonna herself on her knees facing them. They were admitted to her joy. As they prayed, she prayed, adoring the Child which she had laid upon the ground between them, naked on the spread of her voluminous blue mantle. Behind her, they saw St Joseph seated on the saddle taken from the ass, and behind him two shepherds, one of them pointing to the Star in the East. And, as they took in the group with their eyes, they may have begun to wonder if there were not music in their ears, a clear, high sound coming from the little choir of Angels, two of them singing lustily, the others humming as they pick out the notes on their instruments. Sturdy-limbed, standing close together there behind the Child, the Angels have taken possession of the scene, not by any show of wings or other supernatural insignia, only by their purposeful unity of mind and spirit. The scene as a whole could hardly be more natural, with the goldfinch cock and hen confronting one another in the roadway, the irreverent magpie perched on the stone roof of the rude and tumbledown shelter over the manger. Below the other end of the roof the glimpse of Bethlehem, City of David, is very like a corner of Borgo Sansepolcro, the little Umbrian town with the tall towers which lay outside the chapel window.

That Bethlehem and its hills have become Piero's own town of Sansepolcro beside the upper reaches of the river Tiber is not due to lack of knowledge or of imagination in an unsophisticated artist, a 'primitive'. Truly unimaginative was the English 'Pre-Raphaelite' William Holman Hunt when he went in 1854 to paint in Palestine, believing that an authentic background would reinforce the religious message of his pictures. Hunt lost the meaning in informative detail, and in the scenes which he brought back it is the religion which seems incidental. To Piero's fellow-citizens this scene was remote only in the beauty which is revealed in it.

* Throughout the book Roman numerals refer to colour plates, Arabic to black and white.

11. Detail from *The Nativity* (see 1)

They saw in it something like their own countryside; but they saw this with new eyes, found it transformed and purified, apparently by the divine visitation.

The naturalness of this scene, its seeming inevitability will not be the less appreciated if we realise that they are anything but the achievement of a mere observer. It will be worth while therefore considering this particular achievement, examining it more closely, before we involve ourselves in the confusion of largely uncertain facts from which we have to reconstruct, as best we can, the career of Piero della Francesca and discover the factors, no less subject to argument, which influenced it. This picture sums up for us his ideas on life and art, for it would seem to belong to the latter end of his career, to be the result of long experience in acute observation and selective thought, thought clarified by the calculations of a mathematician. For Piero's was one of the great minds of a great period. One of his mathematical treatises, on the geometry of three dimensions, was incorporated wholesale into a more comprehensive work in Italian by a famous mathematician, Luca Pacioli. It was acknowledgment enough, perhaps, in Pacioli's opinion that in an earlier work published two years after Piero's death he had described him as 'the prince of contemporary painting and architecture'.

In his book on the perspective of painting Piero makes it quite clear that he is dealing with only one aspect of the art; and, though we shall come to at least one picture which, now that its meaning has been lost, may seem composed almost as a demonstration of perspective, his mathematics are but a vague clue to the understanding of his art. There are more than enough pictures to show that geometry and painting were to him not at all the same thing. Nevertheless, these parallel interests, occasionally converging, are an all-important clue to the character of the man, and so to the mind and method of the artist. They suggest that in each of these very different arts he was seeking for something which might lie behind them both, for some universal principle which might explain the world of appearances and even the purpose of life. When he came to paint *The Nativity*, though he had no need here of the processes of geometry, his excursions into mathematics must have helped to strengthen and refine his aesthetic sense of balance, his love of order, of clarity, of precision, providing a more or less unconscious discipline when he was laying down the lines of his composition.

To return to the picture itself, one has to admit that since it left his easel it has suffered a great deal of damage, structurally by the splitting into many vertical strips of the panel of poplar wood on which it is painted, but more seriously by the loss of much of its original surface, by the removal of a great deal of paint during some crude attempt to clean it which was made a long time ago. In places, for instance the heads of the two shepherds and St Joseph's hat, almost all the colour has been rubbed away until one can see exposed the gesso, once smooth and white, with which the wood was covered before Piero began to paint in oils. The foreground has been robbed at least of its topmost layer of paint, in which much of the detail was finished; and even in the best preserved part of the main scene, the choir of Angels, the lutes and the primitive violin have lost their strings. Yet, though all these figures with their simple draperies are themselves a good deal worn, they have somehow preserved their look of flowery freshness. While the ground on which they all stand, or rest, no longer seems on close inspection to be quite substantial, in spite of this they remain with all their weight squarely planted on it, permanent, inevitable, as if they could never have been anywhere else. The greatness of a work of art seems sometimes to be almost indestructible, and such is the force of Piero's conception that, after so much of the surface has gone, the illusion which he created is an illusion still, difficult to disbelieve. This world of his creation has remained complete in itself, brighter, purer, stronger than the world we know.

To discover why this picture still makes so profound an impression should be to learn some of the secrets of great painting. It has already been suggested that if Piero did indeed make use of the processes of geometry they would be the least subtle of the means by which this luminous, limitless space has been created and so much meaning imparted to everything within it.

The foundation of this powerful effect is a simplicity which is anything but mathematical. Comparisons are always helpful, and this picture can be compared with one of the same subject and on a similar scale, from which it seems very probable that Piero has taken the theme of his composition: the dramatic contrast of a close-up of the Virgin adoring the newborn Child on a shallow platform of rock before a deep vista of river-threaded landscape in which everything is reduced to the scale of a miniature by an abrupt change of altitude. Alesso Baldovinetti was no more than a dozen years younger than Piero; but his *Nativity* was painted in fresco in the forecourt of the SS. Annunziata in Florence probably some twenty-five years before Piero's. Baldovinetti's *Nativity* also has lost much of its surface, through exposure to the weather; but perhaps the best preserved part of it was always the most charming: that deep, wide plain, close-fitted by Spring with a green carpet sprigged with little trees of deeper green and picked out with little white towers catching the morning sun, all gradually diminishing until they are nothing but dots and dashes of dark and light at the foot of the distant hills. All the ingredients of Piero's composition, including the meagre shelter projected on sticks from the ruinous stone building – something almost as special to both pictures – are already here.

In Baldovinetti's picture the landscape contrast is less dramatic, for the two sun-tanned shepherds awakened in it by the Angel in the sky are not so far below us, and this is the prologue to their reappearance in the foreground on the other side to verify the joyous tidings. But this lack of intensity characterises the whole composition. To look back at it from Piero's picture is to find oneself thinking that Baldovinetti had not more than half comprehended the potentialities of his own invention. His Angels perform a conventional arabesque against the sky. Piero has not only followed the example of the Netherlander Hugo van der Goes in the great triptych which had been set up meanwhile in S. Egidio, the church of the great hospital of Sta Maria Nuova in Florence, and brought the Angels down to earth; he has taken away their wings. This is characteristic not only of his preference for weight over movement but of the concentration which he gives to every theme. He has reversed the proportions of platform and panorama, has selected, simplified, compressed, until everything, animate or inanimate, lends its full spiritual weight to the story, which he has made the same thing as the design. There are hundreds of Italian altarpieces in which the Angels can be seen to sing or strum. This is the picture in which they can be most clearly heard.

Piero's *Nativity* remains original in its integrity, because the greatest kind of originality lies not in the invention of motifs but in the conviction and the freshness with which they are used. For us, as we look at this picture, the Nativity might never have been painted before.

His simplifications are the more remarkable in that during the intervening quarter of a century the Italian painters had mostly followed the path of high fashion which Baldovinetti had been among the first to tread. By this time, for instance, they were usually embellishing their Nativities with elaborate classical ruins. Of course the rude shelter here is much more in keeping than a tumbled Corinthian temple with the simplicity of the Gospel narrative; but this elemental quality is not merely a matter of the details which Piero has chosen to illustrate the story. What other painter would have dared, before the nineteenth century, to fill so large a part of his picture-space with so unattractive and implausible a structure? This crumbling, ungainly building is in fact a simple but powerful device of emphasis and concentration. By its substance and its broad contrasts of light and shade it makes us more aware of the infinite gradations of luminosity in the great sky behind, even while the few lines of its construction are directing our attention towards the drama before it. The comparison with its stony nakedness clothes the participants in an even softer spirit, and its one strong vertical line, reaching almost to the horizontal top of the picture, has the important function of sharply cutting off the landscape vista with its detail made tiny and crowded by the distance from which we look down upon it. Thus by yet another contrast the foreground is endowed with more space and its group of figures with extra significance. Standing with his back to it, the Angel to the left takes over from the wall this function of screening off the world; and he and the other members of the little orchestra, banded close together, form a second shield against it for the Child at their feet. As he lies there beneath them almost in the centre, his ivory body gleaming on the deep blue of the mantle, there can be no doubt that the picture was painted for his adoration; but the mantle beneath him is a part of his Mother, and the shapes of the lutes above him direct us to her, without our knowing it.

As we study the composition these ideas become obvious enough. They cannot in themselves make a great work of art; but the modesty of the human terms in which the picture is conceived accounts for much of the strength of its appeal, and it is only when depth of feeling meets in the same man with an equally powerful and direct sense of form that great art is conceived.

Piero della Francesca's sense of form has its closest parallel, as has often been pointed out, in that of the Greek sculptors of the sixth and fifth centuries before Christ – we know next to nothing of the Greek painters. These carvers and modellers put most of their will-power into convincing us of the strength of their figures, and they succeeded in this not by size and weight of marble or of bronze but by the impression of internal vitality, of contours formed, as it were, from within by the outward pressure of the bones and the flesh and the pulsating blood. It was not movement that mattered to them so much as the power to move; and so there was no sensational violence, no rhetorical gestures, only an extraordinary tension. Their contours did not describe decorative arabesques; they were grandly emphatic, outlining masses equally simple which derive their power from weight, but not from dead weight, from weight which is alive with purpose, with the principle of growth, with the thrust from inside.

In this sense these Angels of the Nativity are Greek, each of them foursquare and all five together making a block as if they had been carved out of stone, or at least conceived by the painter as sculpture. That firm, uncompromising quality of the early Greek figures with their simple planes gives additional value to the few frills that are allowed, to the curls under a hero's diadem or the folds of a girl's taut and diaphanous gown. So here the stony impassivity of these singing boys makes all the more pleasurable the rhythmical, undulating line along the hems of their tunics or, below these, the pattern of the bare feet treading so firmly but so lightly upon the stony ground. It is not only the strong and shapely feet themselves but the shape of the spaces between them that are significant. Again, we are reminded of a Florentine theme, this time of marble choristers from the singing galleries by Luca della Robbia or by Donatello in Florence Cathedral; but Piero's boys are stronger and, above all, in space.

Form and space are inseparable, are part of the same whole; for forms become convincing, seem truly to have three dimensions, only when one is made to believe that one can reach out and feel all round them, that they have room to move in. Every inch of this picture is form, for all the individual forms have space around them and, as one looks at them, one begins to think what a pleasure it would be to move about oneself among them in this clean air. It is more spiritually exciting than that; for Piero, with his greatness of soul, which is hard to distinguish from his abnormally acute perception of form, can impart to such a detail as a piece of drapery something of the grandeur which the ordinary man begins to feel only when he is confronted with things on a scale bigger than himself, with such awesome reminders of nature's power as great trees and rocks or mountains provide. So here in the fall of the Virgin's voluminous mantle, or in the folds of St Joseph's beyond, there are little worlds of form making an impression of greatness which enlarges our souls. As an example of Piero's quiet mastery of the subtle complexities of figure-drawing, look at St Joseph's hands folded so tranquilly on the middle of a shank as he rests one leg upon the other. The foreshortening of this leg is done perfectly, without any of the vulgar emphasis with which some later draughtsmen liked to draw attention to their less sensitive capacities. Indeed, just beneath this passage, the arch of the wooden saddle on which St Joseph sits, with the wooden water-flask tucked into its shade, is a demonstration of the enjoyment that is to be got from the simplest of forms when they are convincingly stated. Just from looking through this cool little tunnel at the warm light on the ground the other side one gets such a profound pleasure as only a master of form seems to appreciate and to be able to impart.

By a mere outline, calling form into existence out of a flat surface, a great artist has the power to quicken our sense of life. He cannot do this without creating incidentally some impression of space. But it seems to be only on a comparatively small scale that outline alone can give complete satisfaction – or perhaps we should have had no sculptors or painters, only draughtsmen. Piero della Francesca must almost certainly have made drawings, besides those on the gesso which formed the actual foundation of his pictures and those which illustrate his treatises in a severely practical way; but we shall see him becoming more and more of a colourist with every picture until, more than any other Italian of the fifteenth century before the Venetian, Giovanni Bellini, who was some forty years younger, he was essentially a painter. In these details of form that have been pointed out the contours are lovely, suggestive, powerful in themselves; but in the fullness of the effect an equal part is also played by the fall of the light, by the warm caresses of the sun on the forms that it reveals, leaving shadows to appear on the other side, cool with the light reflected from all round. And so already in the warm and the cool we have colour, physically inseparable from light, created by light and in turn imparting to the forms which light discloses its own descriptive and enhancing qualities. In any small part of this picture one can discover the key to the special virtue of the whole. The boldness of its design, the simplicity of it are qualities which have belonged to the great masterpieces of Italian painting from its beginnings, from the time, some two centuries earlier, when the painters began to break away from the set pieces of the decayed Byzantine tradition, with their obvious symmetry of design, their surfaces become almost flat. What is new in this picture is the extent to which there is no such thing as mere surface; what matters everywhere is the light, or the reflection of the light. And there is an infinity of light, and so of space, into which one's eye escapes through the frame, right through the wall on which the picture hangs.

Of course this is not a sudden break-through, achieved by Piero in a single moment. The desire to represent space in painting and the power to do so have been growing gradually. Some two centuries before, the great Romanesque painter Cimabue with one or two contemporaries painted forms so powerful that one seems able to feel all round them as one can do actually with a living or with a sculptured figure. But these forms of theirs seem to stand out for the most part against the surface of their background, seem to press it back rather than abolish it; and so do the figures of Simone Martini, the great academic painter in the Gothic style of the early fourteenth century, and his followers in Siena. Before him there, Duccio, the founder of Italian Gothic painting, had almost defied the surface with the atmospheric nuances of his colours as well as the living grace of his line, while the slightly younger Florentine, Giotto, had heralded the Renaissance by introducing the element of perspective. But all these painters used gold backgrounds in their altarpieces, and most of their followers in Florence and Siena relapsed into greater artificiality, with their more florid Gothic stylism. This lasted well into the fifteenth century, right up to the time of Piero's birth. By then, however, the sculptors and the architects of the Renaissance had exploded the old conventions in Florence, and Masaccio was already carrying their new ideas into painting. Perspective had broken through the background as a surface, and the idea that a picture was, first and foremost, a representation of space had firmly taken hold.

But the idea of space is a different thing from the perfect representation of it, the creation of a complete illusion that the frame is not merely a border to a picture surface but a gateway to a world of light and air. In its fullest sense, as an illusion of infinity, this idea of space can be realised only by the depiction of landscape. Landscape painting is a familiar art now, indeed it is perhaps the most popular of all the departments of the favourite art of painting. Every great and growing collection of pictures contains scenes from that brilliant, sensuous, sunny world of the French 'Impressionists' and from that more austere world of the Dutch artists of the seventeenth century, in which cloud and sun are fighting for possession of the panorama below. These are the two great schools of landscape-painting, and the idea of an artist devoting any large proportion of his time to landscape as a subject is scarcely older than the Dutch school. When Piero della Francesca painted his *Nativity* a convincing illusion of the outdoor world was virtually a new ambition.

A walk along the rows of earlier Italian pictures in the great picture galleries reveals that even after the gold backgrounds have disappeared the graceful outlines which were once engraved against them before the colours were applied tend to remain, and that in most pictures the colours are still disposed largely for the sake of balance in a decorative effect. One can understand much of the evolution of painting in Italy up to Piero's time merely by studying the use of a single colour, blue. Blue had always been the favourite hue of the Italian painters. Ultramarine blue – *azzuro oltremare*, 'blue from across the sea' – was their most precious pigment, costlier at times than gold since it was made by crushing and grinding lapis lazuli, a gem-stone which had to be brought all the way from Afghanistan. From time immemorial blue has been the sacred colour, with magical properties, and in Constantinople, when the Byzantine capital was the centre of Christian art, blue became the Virgin's colour, celestial blue, the colour of Heaven. So in the Italian altarpieces before Piero came upon the scene, and indeed for long afterwards, ultramarine blue tends to dominate and to have a special quality, hieratic, in modern parlance 'abstract'. In Piero's *Nativity* blue still predominates; this is a blue picture. Even more thoroughly than usual, his Madonna is draped with blue; indeed, while he was free according to church tradition to paint the gown under her blue mantle red, he has relegated the crimson there to a third undergarment, of which there are only glimpses at her neck and wrist, and over this he has given her a voluminous robe of another blue. Together, the mantle and the gown which cover her almost completely offer two more or less clashing blues, one cool, the other warm. It is St Joseph who has the rose, for his mantle, and the humble shepherds who are clad in the warm colours, toning with the earth, which are needed for the balance of the composition. The Angels are from Heaven, and they too are robed like the Virgin in shades of blue, though these remind us of lavender or lilac or violets, or in white with grey-blue shadows. In the London National Gallery it is worth retracing one's steps from *The Nativity* to the room with the earliest Italian pictures and to almost the earliest of them all, a *Crucifix* by the Master of San Francesco painted two centuries before. Here Christ hangs on a gilded cross which is painted in strong ultramarine blue(!), and the mourning figures at his flanks, less than half the size because they are less important, are mostly, like the Angels of *The Nativity*, clad in varying shades of lighter blue, some of them tending to lavender and lilac. Thus Piero's colouring is symbolic and traditional; but it has come to have a purpose which is virtually new. A comparison with this earlier picture will demonstrate all the more clearly how far its function has gone beyond the decorative. Even in their symbolism Piero's colours are related to the sky. Their quality is essentially atmospheric. What is quite new about this scene of *The Nativity* is what gives the richness and at the same time the realism of its harmony. It is the relevance of every shade of its colour to the whole envelope of the atmosphere. The colours are graded with the utmost subtlety, but not for mere subtlety's sake. Every gradation of every colour plays a part even more significant, if possible, than that of the outlines in fixing the exact position of the object which it is helping to describe in that vast space, itself largely created out of colour-values. Thus the harmony is total. By the union of all the elements in them both art and nature become one.

Unity may be said to be the aim of all artists, and the achievement of all the great. Illusion has been the aim of many base artists, and many have contrived to simulate appearances so as to deceive the eye without achieving any greatness. It is the purpose of the illusion that counts. It is not only the power of the illusion that Piero has created here, the strength of his forms or their unity in space that make *The Nativity* one of the great landmarks in the history of art; for these are cold terms even if they describe the achievement of a great intellect. What we feel in this picture, what we carry away from it, is a great contentment. To those who knelt before it, it must have brought a confirmation of their Christian faith. It must do this now; but it goes beyond the tenets of any particular religion, harmonising the love of God with the love of nature, making them the same. In this way it achieves the aim of the great spirits of the age which has become known by only one of its facets as the Renaissance: the ambition to reconcile the spiritual ideals of Christianity with Antiquity's belief in man's dignity, with the still more ancient love of the natural world. This picture marks a highpoint of happiness, a moment of seeming maturity in the history of man.

2 · Borgo Sansepolcro

The little town that hatched this enlarging genius, Borgo Sansepolcro, lies in the northern tip of Umbria, between Tuscany and the Marches. It is the commercial and agricultural centre of a fertile upland basin, close against the mountain barrier of the Apennines, through which Piero many times in the course of his career would have to seek the high passes eastward. Borgo means, today at least, no more than village; but 'Holy Sepulchre Village', believed to be so called from the character of its relics, has fine straight streets within its walls, and several spacious squares. Churches and palaces solidly built in stone make it no inconsiderable town by any but Italian standards. Much of the Renaissance character which distinguishes it today, however, belongs to times a little later than Piero's. In at least one respect a better picture of the town that he knew is provided now by San Gimignano in Tuscany, a favourite with tourists for the romance of its petrified forest of towers. These were reared by the nobility and the richer *borghesi* of the Middle Ages, first as strongrooms and strongholds, eventually no doubt, like many a skyscraper of today, as symbols of social status. Sansepolcro was no less conspicuous for such towers until the end of the eighteenth century, when they were mostly toppled by an earthquake. The *Torre di Berta*, erected in the twelfth century by the republic and commemorated in the title of the main *piazza*, lasted until World War II, and even today there are stumps of several stoutly built survivors, as well as the grimly powerful fortress of the Malatesta family. This was partly reconstructed in the next century, but it was new and quite up-to-date when Piero was born. The day of the little city republics was then long past. For a century at least, all but the impregnable San Marino had fallen more or less into the power of a succession of despots. Sansepolcro, weakened by plague and earthquakes, had had more than her share, and the town and rich farmlands round about had been Malatesta property off and on from the beginning of Piero's century. Nevertheless, in his youth their fortress became, at least for the time being, redundant, and in the course of his life he must have seen many of the towers demolished, as the times became more peaceful and the idea of town-planning in the classic, horizontal style of Renaissance architecture began to take hold. To the despots every city not essential to their security had its cash value. The Malatesta, who once lorded it over most of Umbria and Romagna, were in decline. Sansepolcro was a long way from their base beyond the Apennines on the Adriatic coast, and they had been obliged to cede it to the Papacy. Now, while Piero was a young man, it was the Pope's turn to sell. Sansepolcro lies only just over the border from Tuscany, and the new owner was the city of Florence, more than ever strongly established as the Tuscan capital.

Owing to the Florentine dominion Piero's times must have been the most peaceful that Sansepolcro had enjoyed for several centuries. There can have been few days when he could not, if he wanted, escape from the intense life of a small town activated by the mercantile genius of the Italians into the fields and vineyards which lapped like a green tide against the walls. It is a landscape which enjoins peace. The river Tiber, which has tumbled from its twin mountain sources not far away and run turbulently for a space, settles down to flow peacefully there through a broad valley, rich with vines and olives and, rarer in Italy, with corn. Today Sansepolcro is the site of a large macaroni factory, and on a few farms agriculture is inartistically up-to-date. In Piero's time, as in Vergil's, and as on most farms today, the pale oxen strained patiently under their yoke at the plough, or at their own leisurely pace bore the produce of the fields and vineyards homeward in the heavy wooden carts. Theirs is the tempo of contemplation.

There is no record of Piero's birth, and one has to guess at the date, which must have been nearer to 1410 than 1420.* His father Benedetto, a tanner and boot-maker, was a citizen of Sansepolcro. His mother Romana came from nearby Monterchi, a few miles off the Arezzo road, which may be why the cemetery at Monterchi now contains one of his most moving works. According to Vasari, who was born at nearby Arezzo a century later, and took pains to collect such memories of Piero as he could, his father died before he was born, and it was his mother who 'helped him in the attainment of that learning to which his good fortune had destined him'. But there is no clue as to what these phrases signify. At a fairly early age he went to Florence, and he was afterwards to paint at several courts; but he was normally resident at Sansepolcro. He was a member of the popular Council there in 1442, when he must have been newly elected and very young for the honour; but he is not mentioned as Councillor again for another thirty-five years. In 1480 he was made Prior for two years of the Guild of St Bartholomew there – his professional association. He was buried at Sansepolcro in 1492. Only one of his pictures, done in fresco at Rimini, bears a date, 1451; and the documentary evidence concerning the rest is scarce and inconclusive. At least there is no record which conflicts with the evidence of character which seems to be offered by his pictures: that of a man who would be faithful to all of the familiar scene that he had learned to love as he grew up, who enlarged his field of action less from restless ambition than from a desire for experience which would confirm his belief in the wonderful diversity of man and nature, and for scope to express the potential harmony between them in images of his own creation.

Even before it was joined to Florence, Sansepolcro probably looked less to Perugia, the capital of Umbria, than to Arezzo, the nearest large town, which is Tuscan and is its link with the Tuscan capital in commerce and in culture. The desire to catch up with Arezzo may well have had something to do with the very first commission which Piero was to receive in his native town. Perugia was a considerable centre; but it was over the hills to the west that the two great schools of painting lay, in Siena and, farther to the north, in Florence. It was to Siena that the Franciscans of Sansepolcro looked for the great picture that they were ambitious to see on the high altar of their church, and the most distinguished Sienese painter of the day, Sassetta, arrived in September 1437 to sign the solemn, elaborate contract. With its many compartments now scattered between the Berenson Collection at Settignano near Florence, the Louvre, the Chantilly Museum near Paris

* Roberto Longhi, *Piero della Francesca*, 1963, pp. 96–107 and pp. 171–92 (Bibliography), gives all the references for these few biological facts.

and the National Gallery, London, this is the most grandiose and elaborate Italian altarpiece of that day.* Its delivery to S. Francesco in June 1444 was the greatest artistic event at Sansepolcro, at least until S. Agostino there a quarter of a century later was endowed with its polyptych by Piero, now likewise dispersed.

But several years before Sassetta had come a second time, to deliver his polyptych, Piero had paid a visit to Florence. He must have heard something, for it was already a generation old, of the artistic revolution that had taken place there, of which there was only a reflection in Sassetta's painting. Perhaps he had heard more of it recently from the painter Domenico Veneziano, who was working in Perugia but was apparently well acquainted with Florentine affairs. At all events, it is in connection with Domenico that we get the first meagre mention of Piero, in a document of 1439. They were then in Florence together. Domenico was engaged in painting *Stories from the Life of the Virgin* on a wall in the Principal Chapel of S. Egidio, the Church of the Sta Maria Nuova Hospital. The records show that Domenico was paid for these at intervals from September 1439 until 1445, and by chance it was scrawled in the margin of one of these accounts that Piero, under the clear denomination of Pietro di Benedetto dal Borgo a San Sepolocro, was with him.† That is all that we are told; and it is thus casually, in 1439, that Piero first appears in history.

---

* Martin Davies, *National Gallery Catalogues, The Early Italian Schools*, 1961, p. 506 and references.
† The references are in Crowe and Calvacaselle, *A History of Painting in Italy*, volume IV, 1911, p. 140, note 1.

3 · Florence and Masaccio

Florence was now one of the great powers of the Italian peninsula. She had acquired a seaport in 1406 when she at last overcame Pisa, which bestrides the river Arno at its mouth and had once sent out fleets which rivalled those of Genoa and even Venice. Florence's own site on the upper reaches of the Arno had no such obvious advantages in security or commerce as those of Venice or Naples or Milan. Nor had she much military genius, though aggressive war with other cities was sometimes a condition of trade expansion or of her very survival. Her power and its gradual extension over Tuscany, her influence throughout Italy and beyond were due mostly to the brightness of her citizens, to their commercial daring and financial flare, their engineering and craftsmanship and, above all, their creative imagination. Their textiles were the finest in Europe and the gold florin, first coined in the middle of the thirteenth century, was standard currency. It has been said that in many an important state Florentine merchants and bankers were almost a fifth column. Their credit abroad, however, was no more remarkable than their stability, in the circumstances, at home. The towers of Florence had once been the tallest and strongest of all, for their owners were constantly in search of each other's blood. Their power had been curtailed in the middle of the fourteenth century, but civil war remained almost endemic, with the control of the nominal republic usually at stake. Yet the merchants and the manufacturers minded their businesses to great effect, organising themselves into powerful guilds, which were incidentally among the greatest patrons of the arts. When markets had to be safeguarded or captured by force, the nobles had their uses, and in the fifteenth century they and the patrician merchants were tamed by the sheer wealth and the outstanding political genius of the great banking dynasty of the Medici.

It was Florentine writers, mostly, who had made Italian, instead of Latin and a host of dialects, the language of Italy, and Florence could already claim to be the intellectual capital. Her predominance in the visual arts was established more slowly; for its diversity, the variety of beautiful species that grew out of the soil of the many independent cities, is one of the wonders of Italian art. In the twelfth and thirteenth centuries it was Pisa which had produced the greatest architects and sculptors, and no mean school of painting followed for a time. At the end of the thirteenth it was two Florentine painters, first Cimabue and then his former pupil, Giotto, who were summoned to Umbrian Assisi and made out of the Upper Church of S. Francesco there the greatest of all the painted monuments of Italy. Giotto's later cycles of frescoes, in Padua and in Florence, were so far ahead of several generations of painters that their seed lay dormant for a century. The Gothic style became universal throughout Europe, and it was to Siena, the one powerful rival of Florence which was left in Tuscany, that Italians must have looked as the fountain-source of style. Now, however, in a few years before Piero was born and during his boyhood, Florence became for a time the indisputable mistress of all the visual arts. She was the birthplace of the Renaissance, and Cimabue and Giotto could be seen as the early prophets of the greatest of all artistic movements since Antiquity.

As you look down on the city from her cypressed hills, you see in the centre, riding on the sea of buildings, perhaps the most living of all architectural forms. The great red-tiled dome of the cathedral seems to rise above its surroundings and to swell out as you look at it, and to hang in the air, eternal as a phenomenon of nature and yet a proclamation of the aspirations and the ingenuity of man. The history of the dome is typical of the Florentine spirit, for the idea of it and its dimensions were decreed by a commission at a time when no one had known for centuries how to span so wide a space. More than fifty years later, the problem was entrusted to Filippo Brunelleschi, who solved it and went on to prove himself the most original architect of the Renaissance. He began to plan it in 1417, and twenty years later saw the cupola blessed, though it was never to be entirely finished, and he did not live to see the lantern which he had designed to surmount it.

The anonymous biography of Brunelleschi, almost contemporary and usually attributed to Antonio Manetti, is one of the first sources in literature for the history of the artistic renaissance, and there is little doubt that the author is largely justified in representing Brunelleschi as its father and the founder-teacher of the new school. We do not need to be told of his mastery of the mechanical sciences and of mathematics, that he could argue with the learned mathematician Paolo Toscanelli, who was his lifelong friend, for his architectural schemes are even more original in conception and in treatment than they are bold in scale. His distaste for the un-scientific vagueness of Gothic building led him to search for the rules of reason which must underlie the architecture of Rome. But there was no trace of pedantry in his classicism; his purpose was to develop a modern style. So there is nothing of the Antique about this dome. It is primarily a revolutionary feat of engineering, a triumph of mathematics. But the mathematics were applied by an architect who was also a sculptor, and one whose sense of form was equal to any scale. Vasari added to 'Manetti's' information the statement that Brunelleschi knew Dante's poetry and studied its 'measures', and we might well make this hypothesis of our own accord when we look at the metrical, lyrical beauty of the little white stone *aediculae* below his dome, with their scalloped niches between the pairs of Corinthian columns supporting the semicircular entablature. The first of the great buildings to be completed in the new style of his invention was the Foundling Hospital, finished in 1424. The airy plan of the '*Innocenti*', with many courtyards, expresses in practical form a large and rational humaneness such as can never have been expressed in architecture before, and the frontal block on the Piazza dell' Annunziata by the poetry of its open arcaded loggia on the ground floor pro-claims an invitation to a new era of peace and trust. The lightness of Brunelleschi's arches, springing straight from his widely spaced and slender columns, gives them a lyrical quality which is completely new. He had no qualms about using iron cross-ties beneath the vaulting of the loggia behind, so that they could support the storey above. The effect was worth it. At right angles to the church of the SS. Annunziata, the '*Innocenti*' is part of a square which Brunelleschi planned. It was only completed in a less inspired form long afterwards, but in the meantime the towers of Florence were to be replaced by houses rationally designed for living and by palaces, proud and almost impregnable still, yet proclaiming by sheer beauty of proportion and ornament a vested interest in the arts of peace.

Brunelleschi was a goldsmith and a sculptor before he turned architect. He also painted two small panels, lost long ago but meticulously described by 'Manetti'. These were views of the two principal squares of the city, done presumably by drawing both plans and elevations and then working them out from these. That of the Piazza del Duomo as seen from the centre of one side, in fact from just inside the great door of the cathedral itself, with the marble Baptistry which fills most of the square confronting it, had at this central point a little hole through the thick panel. Through this, with one eye close to the back of the picture, one could look into a mirror held in front of it and so, from a single viewpoint at a set distance, obtain a complete illusion with everything seen according to a focused perspective system. The sky was silvered, in order to reflect actual light. The second picture showed the Piazza della Signoria diagonally from one corner so that the great stone mass of the historic Palazzo Vecchio, the seat of government, offered itself cornerways in the centre with its two visible façades dramatically foreshortened. There was no hole in this panel, the distance represented on it being too great to allow a mirror to be held far enough away; but the purpose of an illusion was emphasised by the cutting away of the panel at the top along the skyline of the buildings. These were not pictures therefore in the usual sense, designed to show Brunelleschi's prowess in yet another art. They were pictorial demonstrations of a discovery which he had made and which was to revolutionise painting. He had invented the perspective system with vanishing points and a mathematically calculated scale on which the size of everything in the picture diminished according to the distance at which it was seen.* The representation of distance was no new thing in painting. Painters had got a long way with it in the preceding century by empirical means, and no doubt often by calling in the architects when buildings played a significant part in their pictures. But Brunelleschi was the first to work out a correct mathematical system. It was an exciting discovery and, since it was itself a sign of the intellectual resurgence of the age, the sculptors and painters were ready to seize upon it, recognising its potentialities in design.

Head and shoulders above the rest of the painters was Masaccio. Vasari tells us that in his altarpiece with *The Annunciation*, painted for S. Niccoló in Florence, 'there were a house and many columns, admirably painted in perspective', with the effect 'so managed that the colonnade gradually recedes from view in a manner which proves Masaccio's knowledge of perspective'. That picture too has disappeared long ago, but Italian Annunciations without number have survived, which presumably testify to its fame. There is nothing in the story of the annunciation to call for a perspective effect, but from this time for a hundred years and more it seems to have been thought scarcely proper to depict it without some striking feature of architectural recession. Filippo Lippi's *Annunciation* in Michelozzo's church of S. Lorenzo in Florence is an early instance, and the most beautiful of all was to surmount an altarpiece by Piero della Francesca still at Perugia. If Vasari's attribution was correct, it would seem that Masaccio succeeded

* John White, *The Birth and Rebirth of Pictorial Space*, 1957, gives an illuminating account of the introduction of space into Italian painting.

by this means in giving to a story which had been told so often a new and unforgettable dramatic force.

It is possible that even this perspective effect was contributed by Brunelleschi, for there is some evidence that he provided the all-important architectural setting to a picture by Masaccio which has survived. This is the fresco, still to be seen in the nave of Sta Maria Novella in Florence, in which it is at least Brunelleschi's architectural ideas that have enabled Masaccio to give, literally, a fresh perspective to an old theme in order to achieve an altogether new power of expression. *The Trinity with the Virgin and St John and the Donors* is an altarpiece, and beneath the stone altar-table, which may originally have been freestanding, he painted, according to a custom of the time, a skeleton recumbent on a sarcophagus, an *Imago Mortis* grimly reminding the donor and his wife, who are portrayed above, of all that the Trinity should mean to them. They themselves kneel reverently on a painted step above the altar-table, roughly at eye level, on either side of a great vault which seems to open behind and above them, in which is revealed the Trinity, with the grieving Virgin and St John on either side of the Crucifix. That the donors are but mortal, and that what is beyond is miraculous is emphasised again by their being placed outside a tall doorway, with fluted Corinthian pilasters supporting an entablature, all painted to look like an architectural feature on the wall of the nave. It is from inside and behind this that the picture's high barrel ceiling appears dramatically to recede, coffered as in Roman times and rising from an architrave supported by Ionic columns. The light from across the nave seems to strike into this deep chapel from in front and above, revealing the Virgin and St John on their feet by the two foremost columns, and behind the Crucifix, in the centre, the Eternal Father standing on a corniced plinth, perhaps over the sepulchre of Christ, as if to lift up both Cross and Crucified as the Holy Spirit descends. All these figures, mortal and divine, have a massive strength which had not been created since Giotto died almost ninety years before. In Masaccio's fresco we find once more the throb of human life in a glow of light now made more natural by systematic observation. The vault is filled with atmosphere. If their austere concentration did not forbid it, we feel that we could touch or speak to the donor and his wife. Although possibly it was posthumous, for the wife is dressed in black, Masaccio has made of the husband the most powerful portrait which had yet been painted, even more monumental than those, disguised as Saints, by the sculptor Donatello. Donatello came between Brunelleschi and Masaccio in point of age and was thus the second member of the Florentine triumvirate who are hallowed as the founders of the fifteenth-century Renaissance. He too used Brunelleschi's method of perspective in his very pictorial sculptured reliefs, and in the course of his long and prolific career he invented many of the motifs which the painters were to exploit for a generation or more. But the power of Masaccio's portraiture here is not more significant than the revolutionary way in which he introduced these two life-size, secular figures into a religious composition, using them only to emphasise its austerely spiritual character, their motionless reverence adding to the significance of the vision in the space behind their praying hands. In this, everything is rendered in correct perspective except the figures of Christ and his Father. These are not foreshortened, perhaps that they may retain the hieratic grandeur of Byzantine images, made more awesome by contrast with the realism of the steep-

III. Detail from *The Brera Altarpiece*, the Madonna, panel 248 × 170 cms. Brera, Milan

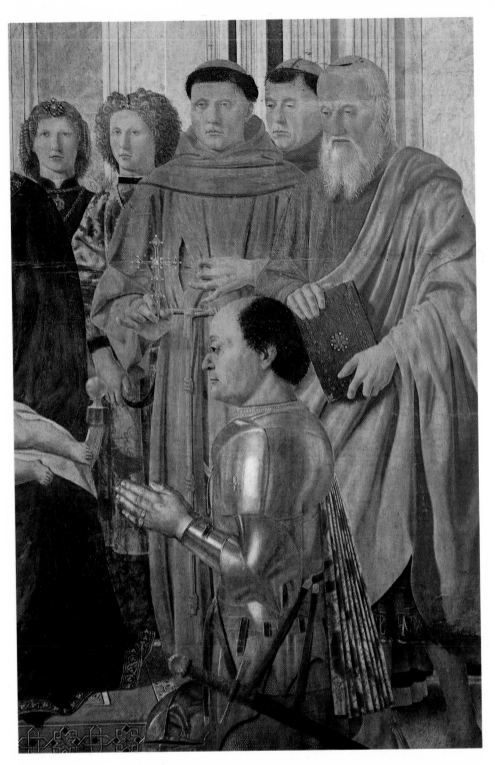

IV

set upward view past the other, apparently foreshortened, figures into the high vault. With the surface of the painting not yet worn and broken and repaired, when such architecture was altogether new and when a complete illusion of solid forms in space had never been achieved before, it must have been an overpowering effect. *

The haloes are gilded; but even they are drawn as discs in perspective, and their gold is the only concession to the traditional use of rich materials. It was not perhaps merely for austerity of appearance that this altarpiece was executed in fresco; but so that it need not be enclosed in a carved and gilded frame. Within such a frame only a very limited degree of illusion had ever been attempted. The typical Gothic-style altarpiece now in vogue had become an elaborate species of screen, with its many separate painted panels enclosed in a complex, richly carved and gilded frame. These pictures were often in several tiers, on different scales. Thus the frame often seemed at least as important as the picture and, with gilded backgrounds to the main panels, a full degree of illusionism was impossible, even had it been desired. In fresco, on the other hand, the medium for epic narrative on the scale of life, painters had always been attempting to make their scenes look as real as they could. They had often framed them, moreover, in illusionist architectural borders which did less to link them as decorative units with the building itself than to suggest by their perspective construction an opening into another world.

Not many months earlier, in the course of 1426, Masaccio had painted for a church in Pisa a complicated altarpiece with panels on different scales which show by their shape that the frame was in the Gothic style, though it has long been lost and the pictures are dispersed. Only a single panel with *St Paul* remains at Pisa; the large central *Madonna* is now in the National Gallery, London, the smaller *Crucifixion* from over it in the gallery at Capodimonte, Naples. In the intensely tragic *Crucifixion* the figures are foreshortened as they would be seen from below. In *The Madonna with Angels* her throne is drawn in correct perspective in the new architectural style. It separates her from the gold background and by its depth allows the light and shade to play over her massive, heavily draped form and that of the Child who, like an infant Hercules, stuffs the purple grapes into his mouth and finds them sour. Nevertheless, with Masaccio's monumental conception in three dimensions the façade-like stylistic convention of the altarpiece is incongruous. He must have determined never to repeat it. It was to fresco therefore, with its tradition of space and realism, that he turned when he painted the first of all altarpieces containing a complete illusion of the divine presence. Since its theme was at least very uncommon, this had no such continuing vogue as that of *The Annunciation* and the influence of the picture is much less obvious. Yet in essence it is the forerunner of all the great altarpieces with figures gathered in a recess, like that painted by Piero della Francesca at the end of his career, now in the Brera Gallery, or Signorelli's *Circumcision* in London, or Giovanni Bellini's S. Giobbe altarpiece in the Accademia at Venice. These may be richer in execution and in the variety of colour and light which a greater number of figures affords. But Masaccio's picture is more than the prototype; it surpasses them all in the

* There has recently been a spate of articles about this altarpiece. John Coolidge's in *The Art Bulletin*, XLVII, 1966, pp. 382–4, is by no means the most definitive; but he gives valuable references and illustrations.

IV. Detail from *The Brera Altarpiece*, Duke Federico II di Montefeltro with Sts Francis, Peter Martyr and Andrew, and two angels daring of its virtuosity. It provides the armature beneath a hundred more sensuous but less solemn compositions. It is the very scaffolding on which the history of Renaissance painting was to be built.

When he painted it, he was probably no more than twenty-five years old. He was certainly not more than twenty-seven when he died, in Rome. Before he went to Rome he may be said to have left in Florence full instructions for the future of painting, in the form of a cycle of frescoes in the Brancacci Chapel of the Carmine Church. Vasari in his *Lives of the Most Eminent Painters, Sculptors and Architects*, published in the middle of the next century, gave a long list of painters and sculptors 'who have become excellent and illustrious by studying their art in this chapel'. He included in it virtually every good painter of the years between, even his great hero Michelangelo, whose marble *Moses* in Rome indeed reminds us, for all its complexities, of one of Masaccio's monolith Apostles. Most of the later men whom the historian lists were actually his own acquaintances, and he would hardly have dared to call them the disciples of so young a man, whose ideas were already a century old, if they had not in fact held the name of Masaccio in deepest veneration.

In documents the name is Tommaso di Giovanni. Masaccio, the nickname bestowed on the painter at an early period, comes by adding to *Maso*, short for Tommaso, the more or less opprobious termination, *accio*, 'bad', or at best 'awkward'. Vasari went out of his way to explain it by Masaccio's carelessness about his own interests and in practical affairs. He was indeed heavily in debt when he died so young. Presumably, in the first place, the name was invented to distinguish him from Masolino, 'good little Thomas', whose career, begun some twenty years earlier, now became interwoven with Masaccio's.

While Masaccio was painting his altarpiece for Pisa, Masolino was in Hungary. It is a generally accepted supposition that, before he went, in September 1425, he had begun to work in the chapel of the Brancacci family in Sta Maria del Carmine in Florence, probably completing the painting of the vaults and the lunettes beneath them. All this, however, was destroyed in the mid-eighteenth century, when the chapel was remodelled. On his return in 1427, Masolino perhaps took Masaccio into partnership for the painting of the chapel walls. What is certain is that at the chapel entrance Masolino painted *The Temptation* on one buttress, while Masaccio on the opposite side painted *The Expulsion from Eden*; that on the three walls each of the two painted a number of scenes from *The Life of St Peter*; that after about a year the scheme was abandoned, to be completed more than fifty years later by Filippino Lippi. The association of the two, one so mild, so sweet, so impersonal in expression, the other so dynamic, so austere, so individual, was perhaps less strange than it seems; for, however much Masaccio may have been befriended by Brunelleschi and by Donatello, who is known to have drawn his pay for him on one occasion at Pisa, he was exceedingly young and in the lonely position of having no equal in painting. It may well have been Masolino who got him employment, and in return Masaccio seems to have broadened Masolino's sense of form and inspired him with an enthusiasm for perspective which was to run away with him sometimes when he was left on his own.

In the Brancacci Chapel Masolino's Adam and Eve are like figures in Gothic painting, their feet not firmly on the ground. They have sensuous beauty and a new simplicity which makes them touching in their nakedness; but they are not

more expressive than that. Masaccio's couple on the opposite wall express the
whole tragedy of the human lot. The foreshortened drawing of the Archangel
hovering in the air with drawn sword, forbidding all retreat, would seem to have
been painted more than a century later, when the Venetians were on the way to
mastering such air-borne effects; but much more significant is the sheer weight
upon the ground of the two primordial figures, heavy with their load of present
shame and future suffering. Linked together as they are in one sculptured group,
each expresses his terrible loneliness in a gesture basic to his sex, Adam covering
his eyes to fend the idea of his children's destiny from his mind, Eve striving to
cover her body as she cries out against their punishment. This gesture of hers has
been traced back to a strangely irrelevant source in the pudic Venus of Antiquity.
At this end of history, the movement was to inspire Rodin to one of his most
expressive bronzes.

Under this pair are two narrow scenes with episodes from *The Life of St Peter*,
painted much later by Filippino Lippi, and the three walls of the chapel itself are a
mixture of work by all three painters. On the short wall with the altar under the
window, it was plainly Masolino who painted one of the scenes, *St Peter preaching*,
for, though the Saint's figure has Masaccio's grandeur, the composition is crowded
and without space, at least in its present state. There is little doubt that Masaccio
painted the other three. But of the four great scenes, each with more than one
episode, on the long walls, only one, *The Tribute Money*, is – except perhaps for the
head of Christ – entirely by Masaccio; in the scene below it he left a large part
unfinished, to be completed by Filippino. On the opposite wall Filippino painted
the whole of the lower scene, while the composition with two episodes over it,
St Peter healing a Cripple and raising Tabitha, is in dispute between Masolino and
Masaccio. With its bold illusion of space and its clear perspective, it is a modern
street scene of no little significance. The figures, however, mostly seem weak for
Masaccio, and it may well be the result of collaboration. In present conditions a
precise definition is almost impossible. This picture is at a considerable height, and
the chapel was always rather narrow for the scale of the paintings. It has been
darkened by a reduction in the size of the window and much has happened to
obscure the appearance of the whole series. In 1771 the church was gutted by fire
and the frescoes are said to have been blackened by smoke. Their subsequent
treatment was unfortunate, for now they look like old oil-paintings sadly darkened
by discoloured varnishes. There is hope that in the near future a thorough cleaning
may restore the luminosity of Masaccio's colour and may incidentally make it
possible to distinguish more clearly between the two hands.

Neither uncertainty about details nor distortion of colour can leave us in any
doubt about the grandeur of the whole cycle. As our eyes become accustomed to
the dimness, we find ourselves in a world as real and human as our own but
peopled by ancestors so grand in scale, so rich in the essence of life that we feel
ourselves unworthy: in our puniness we have let them down. In Masaccio's wide
scene with *The Tribute Money* there are three episodes; but most of the action is
relegated to the two at a distance, one on each side, in which St Peter at Christ's
bidding fetches the coin from the fish's mouth and hands it to the tax-collector.
The great group in the centre stands for sheer grandeur of body and mind. There
is a certain brutal splendour about even the restless importunity of the uncouth

collector; but his figure is designed as a foil to the tranquillity of Christ and the trust of the Disciples, a throng of men majestic in their very impassivity. They stand there weighty as antique statues, but not merely by virtue of the laws of gravity; their feet grip the ground as feet have never done before in European painting, and their motionless stances only emphasise their reserve of power. They see and hear and wonder, while Peter alone is tense and purposeful as he receives his Lord's command. On the right, where he hands the collector his due, are city buildings. While these are based on a diagonal line which points straight to Christ's head, their construction helps to frame this episode apart from the rest. The great space in which the other two take place is the first of modern landscapes. No artificial rockeries here, but mountains looming vast with the mystery of nature as they descend towards the lake, leaving a spacious foreshore in which the throng of men are free to move at will. In the three small scenes also by Masaccio on the short end wall, Peter goes about his mission *Baptising Converts, Giving Alms, Healing the Sick with his Shadow*. His slow, dedicated progress is tellingly contrasted with the eager and desperate attitudes of those whom he assists, with the shivering of a naked catechumen waiting his turn to be douched with water from his cup.

Many of these figures have an extraordinary poignancy, and neither Michelangelo nor Rembrandt was to create a man more impressive than Masaccio's St Peter, especially as he stands intent and singleminded in the great scene before Christ: a man of deep resolves and iron will to execute them. It seems that the bushes of grizzled hair on the massive dome and powerful chin crackle with electricity, and that nothing could distract the clear gaze of those deep-set eyes or deflect the purpose of those broadly sculptured features. It is hard to avoid the term sculpture in describing a head conceived and drawn convincingly in the round with so much breadth and strength; but St Peter is flesh and blood. The light which throws into relief the craggy outlines of his features searches out all those subtle changes of plane which reveal the different tensions of muscle and skin over the noble armature of bone.

The depth of Masaccio's humanity, the keenness of his observation were backed by a will which found means of expression as systematic as they were forceful. If it was Masolino who obtained the commission for decorating this chapel, it was Masaccio evidently who soon came to control the scheme, at least for the painting of the walls. The effect is all one. We feel that above the dado which runs round the chapel there are no walls except those which belong to the various episodes. In some of these there is no architecture, while in those which have buildings our view is never confined as it is in the altarpiece of Sta Maria Novella. All are open to the sky and, for all the physical limits of the narrow chapel, we seem in the midst of nature's infinity. Yet it is all within our focus. Wherever there is architecture it gives us a single vanishing point and a horizon line roughly on the same level as the heads of the *dramatis personae*. And thus we can almost ourselves participate in their performance. Perspective design may be expressionless geometry, but it was avidly taken into the art of painting by the Humanists because it is centred on the viewer, on us. This world of St Peter's and his fellow Apostles may be a more heroic, a more dedicated world than our own. But it does not exclude us. Owing to perspective the painted world is no longer apart, mysterious and hieratic. We are able to become a part of it.

Nevertheless, the rationalism of perspective would have provided but a frigid kind of unity if Masaccio had not combined it with a force which is subtler and more powerful because it is natural and therefore infinitely various, which also must unify if it is faithfully studied, for it comes from a single source. This is the light of day. Owing to the condition of the frescoes we have to make an effort now to see and understand. Originally the light must have come flooding into this chapel, to make the walls vanish as it revealed the brilliant hues in which Masaccio chose to clothe his figures, the lightness of the spaces in which he liked to have them move. The scenes are now browned and oily, the single window has been reduced in size. But at least the opening is still where it was, and it is still the fact that every figure on the long walls appears to be revealed by a light falling from the same direction, as if from the actual source, the window. The fact that the shadows cast by whole figures or by any one part of them upon another all fall in the same direction not only completes the illusion but serves as another great force for unity. At the same time, since no two forms can be in the same place and all the figures are at different angles, as the story demands, no two can receive the light in the same way. Thus the variety in modelling has suddenly become infinite, as are the opportunities of design which nature offers to those who study her. The length of the shadows is measurable, so that those from buildings and from whole figures could in theory have been worked out on the drawing-board like the perspective; but the wondrous variety of chiaroscuro composition which characterises every figure and at the same time gives it place in the whole great lighted space is a miracle of mixed calculation and observation.

The last of the episodes, *St Peter enthroned*, which is probably the last of all Masaccio's paintings, is the most damaged and repainted; yet it may originally have been the strongest in its composition. At the apex of a steep pyramid of monolithic figures St Peter sits *in cathedra* above three kneeling devotees; but he is oblivious of all but the invisible God to whom he prays for even stronger faith. Behind him a great cube of building unites this group with the bystanders under its eaves; and from the shadows among these a single eye, the only one among these scores of pairs of eyes with their dramatic whites, looks straight at us, and through us. Surely this is the searching, questioning eye of the painter, set as it is in a face of brooding intelligence. This is the least conspicuous of many portraits in the lowest tier, each revealing character to a depth never shown in painting before. Man's consciousness of his own individuality and his interest in that of others was of the essence of the Renaissance, and Masaccio expressed it in these portraits with a gravity never to be surpassed.

He and Masolino seem to have packed their kit suddenly and gone to Rome, where Masolino, who survived his junior by at least five years, painted in fresco a chapel of S. Clemente and an elaborate triptych in Sta Maria Maggiore, attributed by Vasari to Masaccio. Some art-historians have thought to find the hand of Masaccio in the main scene in S. Clemente, *The Crucifixion*, and have agreed with Vasari in the case of one panel from the triptych, now in the National Gallery, London; but this is to say that in the fresco Masaccio abandoned his new-found principles of composition and that in the *SS. John Baptist and Jerome* he went back upon the Sta Maria Novella altarpiece, no longer having at his command the weight and gravity with which he had endowed the figures of the Pisa polyptych.

34 One prefers to think that the relative slightness of these pictures is due to their having been painted by another hand; that Masaccio, who must have intended to share these commissions with Masolino, bequeathed his mantle to him, warming him with it, as indeed he has warmed the whole tradition of painting. All the great painters of subsequent generations who have got expression and achieved form by the true study of light and shade have Masaccio as their ancestor.

4 · Masaccio's Successors in Florence

Piero della Francesca stands out so strongly in the line of great painters who are descended from Masaccio that there is a temptation to simplify history and to think of him as the immediate heir. Masaccio has been dead and gone more than ten years when Piero appears in history in S. Egidio in Florence; and Piero was then with the painter Domenico Veneziano. In what capacity we do not know. He has often been carelessly described as Domenico's pupil; but there is no proof that he had anything to do with the painting of the frescoes in S. Egidio and it is certainly not his earliest extant pictures that show a quality of light or a way of handling paint which remind us of Domenico's. Domenico actually came from Venice, as is proved by his signatures, and his mature painting shows the preoccupation with atmospheric colour which later in the century was to characterise the Venetian school. Giovanni Bellini, the founder of the Venetian school of painting, seems to owe much to Piero; and so it is tempting again to simplify, and to imagine Domenico bringing the light of Venice to ignite a torch in Florence which Piero then carried back over the Apennines to the shores of the Adriatic. That would be misleading. In fact Domenico of Venice seems to have learned most of what he knew about colour and light in Florence. His evolution is still an enigma, but the effort to understand it involves the study not only of Masaccio but of at least one of two other Florentines, rather older than himself. Thus between Masaccio and Piero there stands virtually a generation of painters, each of whom was stimulated to exploit in his own way the power to create illusions which Masaccio had bequeathed him.

In April 1438 Domenico Veneziano wrote from Perugia to Piero de' Medici, who was then staying at Ferrara, a letter which strongly suggests that the painter was already familiar with the Florentine scene. In this letter, which is the first documentary record of Domenico that has come to light, he solicits Piero's good offices with his father Cosimo de' Medici, virtual ruler of Florence and greatest living patron of the arts. Domenico is well aware of the competition which he will meet: 'I have this moment heard the news that Cosimo has decided to have an altarpiece made, or rather painted, and that he wants it done in style. I am so pleased with this news; and I should be more pleased still if you could manage, in the goodness of your heart, for me to be the painter. If this does happen, I hope in God to show you something marvellous, even if there are good painters, like Fra Filippo and Fra Giovanni, who already have plenty of work to do, especially Fra Filippo, with a picture which is to go in Santo Spirito . . .'*

Of these two much occupied Florentine painters who were also friars, Fra

* The letter is printed in full in Gaye, *Carteggio inedito d'Artisti*, 1839, volume I, pp. 136–7.

Giovanni, known to us as Fra Angelico, not only was the most important to the story of Piero but probably had been first in the field, though very little is known about his early life. He was christened Guido, and Giovanni was the name he adopted with the Dominican habit. It was not until after his death that he came to be known by the third name, Angelico, which expresses what everyone has always felt in front of his pictures. These tell us clearly enough how sweet and good a man he was, how simple and complete was his faith. These very virtues, however, have caused his true place in the history of painting to receive a belated and still perhaps insufficient recognition from historians. The naïve ideas of Heaven and Hell or of saintly miracles which he chose to depict, his limited success in modelling forms in the round when he was working on any but a small scale caused to pass for a long time almost unnoticed the significance of his achievement in creating a world of light and colour. Indeed the very brightness of his colours, which restorers have been permitted to reveal again, while the almost equally pure colours of his immediate successors have in so many cases been allowed to darken under old varnish or have been veiled by restorers deliberately, has tended to blind his critics to their subtlety and sophistication. His is much more than a technical achievement, more than a new, almost an ultimate summit in the history of striving after luminosity, which has been the ambition of many of the greatest painters. The synthesis of light and colour which he achieved gradually became the essence of an illusion of space, in which men and women who are animate persons are brightly lit and free to move. Neither the spaces nor their inhabitants are as grand as Masaccio's, and the illusion itself probably owes much to Masaccio's example; but Angelico's idealism plays its own highly individual part in the fifteenth-century conquest of nature, in the attainment of that power to create more or less naturalistic illusions which removed all limits from the artist's potentialities of expression or design.

From the beginning he cherished with a scrupulous regard for purity the traditional technique of painting in egg tempera. Or so it would seem. Such statements have to be made with caution, for there are few effects which cannot be achieved almost equally well in either tempera or one of the many vegetable drying oils which were already known to painters at least as potential media. It requires scientific analysis therefore to distinguish the media of old pictures with certainty, and it is only recently, in the London National Gallery, that the necessary means of analysis have been worked out. Nevertheless, since tempera, even if only the yolk and not the whole egg is used, is less likely than oil either to darken with time or to become much more transparent, it would have been particularly well suited to the bright, clear colours and the clean, precise outlines which are the essence of Angelico's methods. His pictures were never less than brilliant.

In the earliest, still Gothic in style, the colours themselves and the relation of one to another have a subtlety which revives the finest moments of the late thirteenth century and the early fourteenth. The palette is enlarged, however, and there are new, bold juxtapositions of one colour with another. From the beginning the best of the Tuscans and the Umbrians used pure colours, shading each not in neutral colour but with the same positive hue, deepened and intensified; or mauve might be used, for instance, to make the shadow in a drapery of light blue. This purity was maintained throughout the fourteenth century, and bold combinations of a more arbitrary nature were invented for the modelling of draperies: mauve

with green or with pink, pink and yellow, green and blue. Angelico adopted these, 37
exploiting many of the combinations used, for example, by the 'Master of the
Codex of St George'. But he used them from the first with a suggestion of atmosphere in their harmony, and with a new degree of sheer luminosity. Then Masaccio
appeared, and Angelico was the first painter who came to understand the new
instrument put into his hands. To him this illusion of light was a joyous instrument
to be wholly dedicated, regardless of the dark, to the proof that all things were
bright and beautiful. He did not, however, understand all the potentialities at once.

Perhaps the first picture in which Masaccio's influence caused a sudden expansion of Angelico's ideas is his *Annunciation* in the Diocesan Museum at Cortona; 6
for here, as in Masaccio's rendering of the theme, a colonnade shown in perspective
gives the scene its depth and much of its dramatic force. But that is almost the
extent, as yet, of the debt. The little building with the colonnade is not very convincing; and to say that the colours of the picture, and particularly the rose –
Masaccio's favourite colour – of the Archangel's tunic, hemmed with scarlet, are
wonderfully bright and pure is not to say that Angelico has yet fully comprehended
the idea of light. The greens of the carpet of flowers, leading back to the hedge of
flowering shrubs and the fruit-trees beyond, may have darkened and gone dull with
age; but this is not likely to be the case with the ultramarine blue of the sky, and
the sky in this scene is not even intended to be the source of light. If it were, it
would still be outshone by the reflections from the gold. Only very gradually could
Angelico make himself forego the embellishments of the old tradition. Indeed, he
mostly increased the use of gold, which he seems to have laid on more thickly than
his predecessors and burnished more insistently. There is a prologue to this scene
in the top left corner of the picture, and there the gates of Paradise are gold, and
the sword of Gabriel who has driven Adam and Eve outside them. In the foreground the Virgin in her mantle of clear blue is seated on cloth-of-gold; the
Archangel's wings and those of the descending Dove are all of gold, only tipped
with colour. The thick metal leaf is endlessly pounced and tooled, to make both
outlines and patterns, so that its brightness shimmers and is never commonplace.
In many parts, to make a transition to the more or less opaque colours, the foil
is overlaid with a coloured varnish, through which it glows ruby or emerald.
Powdered gold also is used, as a pigment, where gilt lines are needed in the hems of
garments and embroidered patterns and in the inscriptions, such as the message
issuing from Gabriel's mouth. All this consummate craftsmanship is not only for
richness of decoration, or even for proof of Angelico's devotion to God. At this
stage in his painting its gleam and sparkle are a great part of the light.

It is only below, on the plinth (*predella*) of the frame, where custom allowed
narrative in a more liberal style because the small scale made the pictures secondary,
that Angelico allowed the light of nature to come into its own. In these *Scenes from
the Life of the Virgin* he has already discovered his genius for pictorial epic. His 7a, b
predella pictures will continue to grow more subtle and bolder in design throughout and c
his life, but the characteristics are already here. An enchanting freshness of vision
is the reward of seizing this new freedom to exploit his love of nature. He clings to
many of the old landscape conventions: the inorganic, disproportionate flowers
and grasses which carpet the whole landscape in the large composition above, the
chiselled rocks of foreground and middle distance. But even these traditional

motifs are painted with a new zest. The artificial hills are modelled in new varieties, the sunlight on their facets making them more convincing; and beyond them are distances born of adventurous observation. The scene of *The Visitation*, with its

dramatic view of Lake Trasimene as it can be seen a few miles from Cortona, is a little milestone in the history of landscape painting. Angelico loves the scenery of Umbria and Tuscany, and in its almost Mediterranean light he renders distance as no one has done before.

He was not of course a *plein air* painter in the sense that Monet was, any more than he was an 'Impressionist' in his treatment of individual forms. The idea of an overriding naturalism, of reconstructing a landscape or a still life for its own sake would have seemed senseless to him. He belongs to a tradition which is religiously idealistic as to every part, as well as to the whole, and his ambition is to bring together in his pictures for the glory of God only exquisite things, pure in colour and clean in shape. Therefore in landscape it was only the distance, where the impurities of life become invisible, that could be painted as it actually appears to the eye. Nevertheless, he came gradually to see in light not only the instrument of brightness but the all-unifying element which would serve him best in creating a harmony. To Angelico, as to all the painters of the fifteenth century, landscape exists as a setting for figures. His own figures are still lit for the most part with the concentrated light of the studio, a studio without glass in its ceiling. But they are so brilliantly, so purely coloured that they seem to increase the intensity of the light in his outdoor scenes. Under the blue sky of these he established a convincing harmony which entitles him to be regarded as one of the pioneers of landscape painting.

If Angelico was not famous already, *The Annunciation* at Cortona must have made him so. He soon needed several assistants in his workshop, if only to produce the variants of this theme which were ordered for other places. A splendid example is in the Prado Museum. The Dominicans of Brescia ordered an Annunciation of him in 1432. If only this had survived, or could be identified, we might have had an approximate date for the Cortona picture. It can only be presumed that it was painted later than Angelico's triptych, *The Virgin and Child with Angels and four Saints*, in the same Museum, which shows no trace of Masaccio's influence.

This is recognised by most historians in the one panel-painting by Angelico on the monumental scale, commissioned of him in 1433 and now, together with most of his extant work, in the Fra Angelico Museum of S. Marco in Florence. It is a folding triptych, the large round-arched panel in the centre occupied by a life-size *Madonna* seated full length, the wings forming a pair of doors which can be closed over the *Madonna*, each painted on both sides with a standing Saint. It comes from the hall of the Guild of Linen-Manufacturers and Drapers, who paid a price for it which shows that Angelico was famous. In return he contracted to use 'inside and out the best and finest gold and blue and silver that are to be had'. The whole, in its gilt wood frame, is set in a tabernacle of white marble, carved and partly coloured and gilt, which had already been commissioned of the sculptor Lorenzo Ghiberti.

Ghiberti had been the most famous decorative sculptor in Florence from the beginning of the century. In 1401, over the heads of Brunelleschi and others, he had won the competition for the commission to make the second pair of great

bronze doors for the Baptistry; he was to make a third pair later on. In the meantime his Florentine workshop provided the first training of many artists who were
to become famous, most of them as sculptors but several as painters. Ghiberti's
forms, with their combination of lively study from nature in the round, which was
modern, with a linear grace in the folds of elaborate drapery, which was still
Gothic, seem to have been a constant influence upon Angelico until amost the end
of his career. There is no documentary evidence to support it, but the suggestion
has often been made that he too may well have served his apprenticeship under
Ghiberti; for in the altarpiece of the Linen Guild the principles of Ghiberti may be
said to have been translated into painting. In the *Madonna* panel, of which more
than half the surface is gilded, the great loops of the draped curtains are like
Gothic sculpture, seeming to have the weight of the metal itself. The *Saints* have a
majestic power which is indeed reminiscent of Masaccio; but the folds of their
draperies maintain the Gothic rhythm in their graceful curves. These could well be
claimed as the last great Gothic figures in Italian painting. Masolino is known to
have been the pupil of Ghiberti; and he and Angelico have so much in common
that a comparison of their works would be rewarding.

Masolino leaves a much less clear and compact impression than Angelico; but,
just as today the concentration of Angelico's work in S. Marco gives an impression
we cannot obtain of any other Renaissance painter, so in his lifetime there must
have been great advantages in a consistent monastic career. His own monastery
was that of S. Domenico, outside Florence on the way up to Fiesole, and it is here
that he must long have had his studio, painting many pictures, now mostly dispersed, for S. Domenico itself, and sending others to Dominican convents throughout Tuscany and Umbria, even to Brescia, as we have seen. The Dominicans then
came under the ubiquitous patronage of Cosimo de' Medici. For the observing
members of the Order he succeeded in obtaining the obsolescent monastery of
S. Marco in Florence and had it entirely rebuilt by Michelozzo in the new style.
As soon as possible, Fra Angelico and his assistants must have set up workshops at
S. Marco; and they continued to work there for many years. They painted some
sixty frescoes, including a scene in each of all but one of the fifty-five cells.

The church of S. Marco was also remodelled, the principal chapel being completed and probably in use by 1439. Angelico painted the high-altarpiece. No
record has survived of any contract; but plainly this could be the commission
which Domenico Veneziano had so much wanted the year before. The altarpiece
is now in the Museum; but so much of its surface has been lost and so brown a
varnish only lately added, presumably in an effort to conceal the fact, that all its
brilliance and much of its depth have gone. It is difficult now to realise how daring
was the composition, which exerted a great influence on a generation and more of
Florentine painters.

The altarpiece of the Linen Guild was by no means the last of the great multiple
altarpieces with the Madonna and the Saints isolated in separate compartments;
but Angelico had already broken quite new ground in another altarpiece, now in
S. Marco but painted for the Dominicans of S. Vincenzo d'Annalena. Here already
he had put everything onto a single rectangular panel, grouping the Saints together
in one wide scene, three on each side of the Madonna. In the high-altarpiece for
S. Marco he went further, setting the enthroned Madonna deep in a wide scene, so

that she and the Child are almost encircled by the large company of Saints and Angels. He could not forego the screen of cloth-of-gold; but this has been carried into the open air to protect the divine company from the breeze which might blow through the trees behind; and originally, when the sky was blue and the light brilliant, these cool airs must have been almost sensible. Indeed, in the two *predella* scenes from this altarpiece which are preserved in S. Marco it can be said that perhaps for the first time the light is regarded as paramount and that the colours have been restrained and harmonised in order to achieve a convincing atmosphere.

In 1447 the master himself was called by the Pope to the Vatican. This must have been the climax of his career. He took with him several assistants, including Benozzo Gozzoli, who seems previously to have been working for Ghiberti and who later became famous for his cheerful, mundane wall-paintings in the chapel of Cosimo's new palace in Florence, now known as the Palazzo Riccardi. After two years Fra Angelico had to go back to S. Domenico to serve as Prior; but at the end of his three-year term he returned to Rome. There he died in 1455.

The greater part of his work in Rome was destroyed long ago; but the complete fresco decoration of the little private chapel of Pope Nicholas v in the Vatican, with its cycle of *Scenes from the Lives of St Stephen and St Lawrence*, has survived more or less intact. All the painting that he did for the greatest of the Dominican convents in Florence, Sta Maria Novella, has been destroyed. Nevertheless, perhaps more than half of his work has survived, much of it in good condition, to be reasonably well cared for today. In this we are lucky, for it is far from the case with many Italian painters of the first half of the fifteenth century.

Fra Angelico is the least sculptural of all the great Italians. Only in the Linen Guild triptych did he come near to the monumentality of a Masaccio or a Piero. But the surviving frescoes in the Vatican show him capable of composing wall-paintings with figures in almost life-size, beautifully related to each other within a framework of contemporary architecture, about which he had no doubt learned something from Michelozzo in S. Marco. His forms on this scale, however, seem a little thin and dry. In the privacy of the cells of S. Marco, where the Dominican rule had encouraged him to bring home to a single Brother in the simplest terms the full meaning of the Transfiguration or the Ascension, the lack of monumentality is of less account. Here, because he put aside style and convention and gave full reign to the fervour of his faith, his design sometimes touches the transcendental. There is no time or place in these cells, only a single everlasting moment from the New Testament story.

These inward visions dedicated to private devotions may well have been seen only by a handful of contemporaries. It is Angelico's pictures on panel, therefore, to be seen in places of general worship, that exercised an influence on the history of painting. The qualities of his *predella* pictures are developed on an altarpiece scale in the large *Deposition from the Cross* in S. Marco, for Sta Trinita in Florence, with its open landscape ending in an idealised fifteenth-century Jerusalem of pink and white houses roofed here and there with black. The consummate gracefulness of their grouping cannot disguise the lack of weight and articulation of the many figures. Nor can these be explained merely by the intervention of assistants. This is one of those pictures in which the weakness of the parts is forgotten in the beauty of the whole and in the pathos of the expression. The tenderness of the

actions and gestures of grief is made intensely poignant by the rendering of the
natural beauties of the world renounced, of the eyes in the wonderfully tender face
of the dead Christ, closed for ever to the joyous brilliance of the light.

In this comparatively late picture it can be seen that the delight in detail did not
impede the continuous development of Angelico's design. That he could almost
perfectly control it is shown by an altarpiece in which he developed further the
idea of the *Madonna d'Annalena*. This, also now in S. Marco, was commissioned by
Cosimo for Sta Buonaventura at Bosco ai Frati, near the Villa Medici at Caffagiolo.
Cut presumably at the top, but otherwise well preserved, the panel must be counted
as a landmark in the history of composition. Again, the simple but grandiose architecture, with the broad, high central niche giving room for Angels to stand beside
the throne and the screen enriched with pilasters and little scalloped niches extending on either side, still falls short in itself of the monumental. So do the Saints,
standing three to either side, though they are portraits of living, breathing personalities, the consummation of Angelico's lifelong practice in portraying members of the Dominican Order whenever they could be squeezed into a decorative
scheme. Nevertheless, the architecture is noble, and its absolute symmetry is just
what is needed to give an eternal value, an immutability to these individuals
grouped with a new naturalness under the luminous heaven. Palms and fruit-trees
behind the screen almost shut out the sky; but we should know it was there from
the quality of the space alone. There is no space without light. Here the space is
clear and formal. Within it, one might almost say by it, Angelico has given expression to the humanistic religion of the preaching Orders in a profound unity of
form and colour and light. Moreover, his new appreciation of the value of half-
tones, of the beauties of reflected light, gives this picture an immediately important
place in the development of the art of painting.

Fra Filippo, the other Florentine painter mentioned by Domenico in his letter to
Piero de' Medici, had so little in common with Piero della Francesca that he can
have played at most only an incidental part in his history. He was baptised Filippo
Lippi, the names by which he is generally known, and was unconventional in not
changing his Christian name when he took his vows, in 1421. Perhaps he took
these less seriously than did Fra Angelico. Vasari's statement that Filippo had been
placed in a monastery as an orphan and a charity boy could have been invented in
order to excuse the tales which he goes on to tell of his amorous adventures.
Nowadays these are passed over as gossip; but Fra Filippo had an acknowledged
son Filippino, who was also a famous painter, and certainly in Filippo's pictures
one may look in vain for the piety of an Angelico. They were all painted perforce
for devotional purposes; but they give the impression that he would have been
much more at home with the subjects of Catullus or Ovid. He should have been
born a generation later, for during most of his lifetime love and romance were
considered suitable only for furniture painting.

He belonged to the Carmelite Order, and the church of his monastery in Florence,
where he daily made his devotions, was the very church, Sta Maria del Carmine,
in which Masaccio had painted the famous frescoes which Filippino was to complete. Filippo is first mentioned in the records of the Carmine as a painter in 1431,
and it must have been at about this time that he painted his earliest surviving work,
a much damaged fragment of fresco depicting *The Foundation of the Carmelite Order*.

It is now in the Belvedere Museum, Florence. This shows him striving to be a worthy successor to Masaccio. It has massive figures, surprisingly mature, in a massive, austere landscape, strongly lit.

Soon after this, however, he seems to have left Florence and begun to move about freely in search of employment for his brush. In 1434 he was at Padua, painting frescoes in the great Franciscan church there, 'the Santo'; but of these there is not even a fragment. He next appears in Tarquinia, some fifty miles north of Rome; at least, it is from there that was brought to the National Gallery in Rome the *Madonna and Child* signed by him and dated 1437. The same year he was back in Florence, and commissioned to paint the great altarpiece for Santo Spirito there which Domenico mentioned in his letter; he did not finish it until 1443 apparently. It is now in the Louvre.

In both these tempera paintings on panel there is little trace of the solid, sculptural vision of his early fresco. Instead, there is apparently a dashing virtuosity, though the subtlety of his technique, with its tempera(?) glazes, and the sheer complexity of his design, must in fact have involved a slow process of execution. In all his pictures Filippo draws the architecture of the new style with more dramatic and decorative invention than understanding. His figures, even when sitting or standing, seem full of restless movement, their draperies bunched and swirling luxuriantly about them. He used almost as much gold as Fra Angelico; but in another, softer way, while his principle of colouring is altogether different. Sometimes, indeed, he uses a variety of brilliant hues; but more often he eschews bright near-primary colours and uses rather murky hues, rose to dull purple being often set off by a kind of terracotta. These are not contrasted so much as fused into turgid softness by the admixture of black and white. There are subtle shadows; but in comparison with the bright noontide of Fra Angelico, the light in Fra Filippo's pictures seems to have been filtered on a hot afternoon through shutters into an indoor world.

As it happens, one can see the work of Fra Angelico and Fra Filippo together in a single picture, the disc (*tondo*) with *The Adoration of the Kings* in the National Gallery, Washington. They do not seem to have collaborated, exactly, for there is no effort to disguise their individual styles. It would seem that Fra Angelico designed the picture as a whole, for the buildings and most of the landscape are characteristic of his crisp style, with clean facets to the forms and frank contrasts of colour in the clear light. We can recognise as his the three members of the Holy Family, together with most of the distant figures at the foot of the buildings which mount the hill to the right. We can even recognise the hand of one of Angelico's assistants in the exotic birds and the dog in the foreground, together with the carpet of grass and flowers upon which he lies. But, further back, the rickety stable and those unconvincing little steps of rock surrounding it are characteristic of Fra Filippo, who was not much interested in landscape. So, above all, are the Kings, with their long train of rather childish personalities. Even the leading King, who kneels to touch the Child's foot, looks like a sulky little boy provided with too much beard and whiskers for a Christmas play. The many-coloured throng behind are not in the bright light like Fra Angelico's Holy Family; they seem to be indoors. Presumably Fra Angelico left the picture unfinished, perhaps when he went for the first time to Rome.

It would be quite unfair, of course, to estimate the value of the two artists by this comparison. Fra Filippo plainly had little or no part in the design of the *tondo*; and he was an original and exuberant composer. Fortunately, there is also in the same National Gallery one of his most forceful compositions: *The Annunciation*, probably painted in the 'forties for the Palazzo Vecchio, the seat of government in Florence. Even here the two figures are strangely proportioned and waywardly childlike, and, as in most of Filippo's pictures, the hands, so unlike the expressive hands of Fra Angelico, are blunt-fingered and insensitive. But as a whole the figures are solid and even grandiose, like the strongly designed, four-square section of a building in which they meet. If the picture indeed came from the Palazzo Vecchio in Florence, it was almost certainly designed as an over-door. It would thus be meant to be seen from a distance and this would explain the unusual simplicity and carrying power of the design. More than any other panel by Filippo Lippi it reminds us of Masaccio, not by any nobility in the figures but by the way in which the perspective is organised and the light takes possession of the scene. The highlights of the turbid colours are dusted with gold. Everything glows darkly in it and, as the light slowly discloses the drama, we are aware of its creative power.

Fra Angelico worked almost exclusively for the Dominicans, and even before his departure to Rome Filippo Lippi must have become the fashionable painter in Florence, enjoying above all the patronage of the Medici. Nevertheless, from 1452 Filippo worked a good deal at Prato, where the only mature frescoes from his hand are preserved in the cathedral, and where his son Filippino was brought up. They were working together from 1467 at Spoleto, where Filippo died in 1469. In the frescoes at Prato his figure-painting with its decorative linear rhythms smothered in the swirl of gauzy, delicately coloured draperies is seen in full scale in its maturity. This sensuous style, with its emphasis on fashion and romance, plays only a subsidiary part in history, as foil to the heroic tradition of which Piero is the culmination. If any link is needed between Fra Angelico and Piero della Francesca, it is to be found rather in Domenico Veneziano.

Though it was probably Angelico who got the commission for which Domenico was angling in his letter of 1438, it is possible that Domenico did not solicit the patronage of the Medici in vain. He promised, if he were given such a commission, to show wonders, and it could be that the *tondo* with *The Adoration of the Kings* now in the Berlin–Dahlem Museum is a wonder-picture produced by Domenico for Cosimo de' Medici or his son Piero as proof of his virtuosity. The *tondo* may possibly have come from the great palace in Florence, designed for Cosimo by Michelozzo soon after Domenico's picture is likely to have been painted.

In any case his *Adoration* must have been produced with the intention of surpassing the Gothic altarpiece of this subject, now in the Uffizi Gallery, which Gentile da Fabriano, coming from Venice, had completed for Sta Trinita some fifteen years before. Less an altarpiece than a pageant of Northern chivalry, with ladies-in-waiting for the Virgin and for the Kings an endless train of knights equipped for all forms of the chase, not so much a painting in the Tuscan or Umbrian sense as a heap of treasure, glittering with ornaments embossed above the painted surface and glowing with translucent colours laid over gold and silver leaf, it had set all Florence agog. There are echoes of it in many subsequent Florentine pictures of greatly superior design. Angelico must have borrowed some of his ornamental techniques from it; neither he nor Filippo can have forgotten it when they were at work on their *tondo* now in Washington.

Domenico's, however, was painted probably before theirs. Gentile had come to Florence from Venice, and Domenico, who was a native of Venice, must have felt a particular interest in the altarpiece by which Gentile had acquired such fame. It has even been suggested, reasonably enough, that he had come to Florence in the first place as Gentile's pupil or assistant. By now, however, he was the rival, not the imitator, of Gentile, surpassing him not only in the extremity of sartorial fashion displayed by his kings and their retinues but in the up-to-the-minute manner of his painting. For all its fantasy his *Adoration* is wholly of the Renaissance. The Holy Family themselves are strongly reminiscent of those in the *predella* scene, now in Berlin–Dahlem, from Masaccio's Pisan altarpiece; the Kings and their train, for all the small scale, are not types of chivalry, like Gentile's, but each one distinctly, intensely, individual. The landscape is a garden of delights, its foreground carpeted with flowers, its stable neat as a summerhouse, with a peacock superbly hanging its great tail from the roof over the Virgin's head, its distance closing mistily with mountains rising from the waters of a lake. One can wander in this little world for ever, finding new pleasures for the eye. Yet, if it is artificial, this is mainly in its idealism. It unfolds itself from foreground to far horizon naturally, convincingly, and each of the forms in it has its proper weight. Unlike Gentile, Domenico has remained in control of his own creation. True, he has not arranged his throng of figures to fill the circle with its pattern, as Angelico was to do; he stretches it in forthright fashion straight across. But he has made full use of the circular shape, which may well have been his patron's choice, to hold a world of forms of every description in focus for our enjoyment.

By September 1439 Domenico was at work painting the first of three frescoes on a wall of the Principal Chapel in S. Egidio in Florence, where we first hear of the existence of Piero della Francesca. To Domenico himself payments for work in S. Egidio continued erratically into 1445. Even then he seems to have left one scene at least with some figures unfinished; for in 1461, the year of his death, indeed not long before it, Alesso Baldovinetti was apparently contracting to finish the scene with *The Marriage of the Virgin*. Meanwhile, the opposite wall had been completely painted by the dynamic Andrea del Castagno. This consequently became one of the most important cycles of wall-painting in Florence, still much admired in the following century in spite of drastic changes in taste. Yet, probably before the end of it, it was destroyed for the sake of 'improvements'. Some twenty years ago the remaining fragments were uncovered, and some are now in the Belvedere Museum, Florence. It would be dangerous to make deductions from what they seem to tell us of Domenico's style.

Most of his other works have suffered a similar fate, and it is impossible to know whether Domenico was a great inventor or largely an eclectic. We have no certain dates either for the frescoes by him of which fragments survive in the National Gallery, London, and in Sta Croce in Florence or for several Madonnas. Of these the finest, and the most important, for the Virgin is in full length, is *The Madonna enthroned before a Rose Hedge*, now in Bucharest. Here the impact of Florence is evident in reminiscences of both Masaccio and Filippo Lippi; but Domenico has given much in return. This tall figure seated on a metal chair, with upright back and feet planted squarely on the ground, may be early enough to have inspired many Florentine Madonnas of the next generation. The picture is much darkened by dirt and old varnish, so that the colour has to be guessed at. Almost certainly it was always darker and less sophisticated and the drawing more powerful and elaborate than in the *Madonna before a Rose Hedge* in the National Gallery, Washington, a picture on a larger scale but with the Virgin only in half length. In the interval Domenico seems to have been converted to the atmospheric colour of Fra Angelico. The Washington *Madonna*, with her corn-gold hair and colours which remind one of flowers in a garden in the early freshness of a bright Italian day, must be closely related to the one great altarpiece from Domenico's hand which has survived, from which two little *predella* pictures are also in Washington and two in the Fitzwilliam Museum, Cambridge. This is the signed *Virgin and Child enthroned, with four Saints* from Sta Lucia in Florence, now in the Uffizi Gallery.

Though it is more likely to have been painted about the same time as the altarpiece from Bosco ai Frati, Domenico's St Lucy altarpiece derives more obviously from Angelico's earlier picture from S. Vincenzo d'Annalena, with the Madonna's throne brought forward in front of an arcaded screen, which holds the composition together. Curiously enough, Domenico seems to be attempting, perhaps under orders from his patron, to preserve something of the Gothic tradition. At least its ghost may be said to have survived, for the picture-plane is divided by three arches pointed at the top. Moreover, though these are the arches of an airy marble arcade which runs across the picture, the Madonna's throne is placed exactly under the vault of the centre arch and the Saints stand aside from it in two groups under the other arches. Beyond them, however, the white marble columns are faced from the back of the scene by an elaborate piece of Renaissance architecture, a five-angled screening wall of marble with three niches and on either side an archway into a slender loggia.

But what lays the ghost of the old tradition is the light. With its help Domenico has created one of those rare scenes which, for all its complicated structure, we are able to comprehend at first sight and to accept instantly as a whole. Indeed, we seem almost to be drawn into it, made free of its space, bathed in its atmosphere. The experience is never forgotten. Not that the lighting itself is simplified. We are made immediately conscious of the daylight here as we are not in any of Angelico's large pictures. As if determined to show its good intentions, the almost excluded sun throws a great triangle of brightness across the coloured marbles of the wall behind, while the orange-trees which it has brought to fruit testify on its behalf by displaying their topmost boughs elegantly above the cornice, one over each recess. But most of the light is of necessity reflected light. The whole scene is alive with action and reaction of light upon colour and colour upon light. The pale bright colours in which the Saints are arrayed, greens and yellows and blues and rose of every shade, set off by patches of scarlet, become deeply intensified in the shadows of the folds of their draperies. In this flower-coloured world only St John Baptist's tunic of brown camel-hair seemed alien; so Domenico touched all the high-lights with silver – or white gold.

The composition is thus more ambitious than any of Angelico's, an attempt to deal with greater complexities of space; but these, unlike Angelico, who perhaps knew better what he was able to do, Domenico has failed to master. Only if one takes seriously the invitation to enter these marble halls which is so gaily proffered, and looks again at the architectural design which holds together only in its surface pattern, does one make the discovery that much of the space is not really there. Above all, the marble decoration which at the top forms the frontal picture-plane belongs to a wall supported by columns which towards the bottom are seen to have their bases behind the Saints, deep in the picture-space. When the effect is so charming, the very atmosphere so convincing, it may be asked what more is necessary. The answer is best found in the mature pictures of Piero della Francesca, who brought to this idea of painting an exact science in the construction of three-dimensional effects. He was to prove that this is the means to a much greater power of expression, to a harmony even more profound.

5 . Piero's First Picture

While the first document mentioning Piero della Francesca merely states in 1439 that he was with Domenico Veneziano in Florence, the second records in 1442 his membership of the City Council of Borgo Sansepolcro. It was in 1441–42 that the Pope, to whom the little town had belonged for many years, sold it to Florence. Whether there is any significance in Piero's appearance on the Council in the year when the city became Florentine one can only guess. There may have been none. On the other hand, our knowledge that at least he had been in Florence makes it seem possible that he was either nominated by the Florentines or elected by local interests as someone who had contacts in the capital. In either of these cases it would follow that he must have spent enough time in Florence to have made himself known there. Apart from that question, his election suggests that he was now a person of some standing. This can hardly have been as a painter; no contemporary written reference to artists as yet includes any mention of him, and there is no evidence so far concerning any picture by him. For this we have to wait another three years.

His story as an independent painter begins at Sansepolcro in January 1445,* with the contract to paint the complex altarpiece, a polyptych, of which the pictures themselves are preserved in the Gallery there. The contract was with the Confraternity of the Misericordia, a charitable organisation still to be found in every Italian town; and in what was once the centre panel of the main tier, larger than all the rest, the *Madonna della Misericordia*, 'the Virgin of Mercy', towers over a group of kneeling devotees, one of them hooded in black as are the members of the society when they are caring for the dead.

Y-XIV
23

There was nothing new in this theme of the Madonna sheltering her little well-dressed brood under the wings of her cloak. Invented probably some two centuries before, it had become increasingly popular in the last hundred years, since the great plague which had decimated Europe. In general it had been a subject mostly for modest sculptures and paintings by rather obscure artists; but this was not so in the neighbourhood of Arezzo, at least since about 1400, when a locally famous example had been painted by Parri Spinelli, son of Spinello Aretino, the prolific late Gothic painter who was well-known throughout Tuscany. Parri had painted it on the wall of an oratory erected by the followers of Bernardino of Siena. The future Saint had taken strong objection to the time-honoured practice of certain pagan rites at a spring which gushed from the base of a green hill just outside the town, and had brought a band of zealots to block it up for ever. The oratory which they built as a diversion became a place of pilgrimage, largely it would seem owing to the popularity of Parri Spinelli's great picture. In 1444 Bernardino died, to be venerated immediately as a Saint, and for Parri's *Madonna della Misericordia* (though the fresco

9

* Longhi, *op. cit.*, pp. 19–24 and 97–8, gives all the references. He believes that the payment in 1462 to Marco della Francesca was for this altarpiece (see below).

had to be cut to accommodate it) the studio of Luca della Robbia in Florence was ordered to produce the most sumptuous of Renaissance frames. Richly modelled swags of fruit in enamelled terracotta form a coloured border within a great black and white triumphal arch carved in marble. Among the four Saints carved in full relief on the face of the arch is S. Bernardino. This high-altarpiece was the glory of the church of Sta Maria della Grazie which rose in place of the oratory.

The altarpiece ordered from Piero at Sansepolcro was plainly the result of the same movement. Here too Bernardino, though not yet canonised officially, is one of the four Saints who were to stand two on either side of the *Madonna della Misericordia*. It is always both fascinating and instructive to compare Piero's treatment of a theme with that of his local precursors, with which he can often be seen to have been familiar, however much the theme has been transformed in his hands. In Parri's picture the score of kneeling worshippers are much like a close-packed crowd in any Gothic fresco. Here, though local worthies occupy the front places (also with a black-cowled member of the society in the second rank), Pope and Emperor are included to show that the theme is universal; and over the heads of the throng, above the level of the Virgin's waist, there reigns a balanced regularity of design which leaves no doubt about the hieratic intention. This might be a Byzantine mosaic in an apse. The encircling white mantle, lined with red and starred with red and gold ornament, is draped like a pelmet from the great arc of the extended arms, and from the horseshoe of its collar the turned column of the neck rises to support a head which is oval as a *mandorla*, with unseeing eyes turned neither up nor down but levelled into space. The halo is a disc, flat on the background, emphasising the symmetrical design of crown and hair and head-veil; and on either side two Angels swing their censers in attitudes which are exactly reversed. Piero in his centrepiece has accepted completely the idea of remoteness and universality suggested by a symmetry which is almost absolute. Indeed, his Madonna brings to mind a prototype from even farther East in some enthroned Buddha, carved with austere simplicity in India or China a thousand years before, with eyes benevolently turned down, as hers are, upon the worshipper. Yet this sculptural quality and the extreme simplicity of Piero's representation distinguish it emphatically from Parri's calligraphic and highly decorated design. The halo has become a floating disc seen in perspective from below, and at the base of the monolithic figure robed in brilliant crimson the shoes of another red are planted firmly on the almost black carpet (once dark green, presumably) covering the marble plinth. The long mantle of a peculiar greyish blue is heavy and lined with thick grey fur, and within the half-light of its folds there is ample room for the four men and the four women who are gathered in its shelter on their knees. These are not types outlined on a rich surface, but individuals eager for attention, solid figures in space, to each of which Piero has given the kiss of life. The remoteness of the Madonna and the immediacy of the light combine to make them seem touchingly conscious of their mortality. Thus, while Parri's picture is a highly decorated surface, Piero's is a rather stark and dark illusion in three dimensions.

Alas, the group of pictures of which the *Madonna della Misericordia* was the centre is now without the feature which originally held it together, the presumably elaborate carved and gilded frame. In the contract Piero had promised to use fine gold and fine colours and especially ultramarine blue, to paint the pictures himself and to complete them within three years; he also promised to inspect the altarpiece at intervals and gave a ten-year guarantee for both the structural work and the painting. Though the frame itself is gone, the six little pictures of *Saints* have survived which were once set in pilasters, and so have the five little *Scenes from the Life of Christ* which were part of the *predella*. These are by another hand. Evidently Piero was free to let a subcontract for these accessories to an independent painter.

This subcontractor was evidently more of a professional than Piero was as yet. Painted apparently in the traditional tempera technique and without hesitation or inconsistency, his figures and his compositions have survived in better state than those of the great man. His scenes are lively in design, their colours brilliant; but one gets the impression that his talents would not have reached to a much larger scale. Perhaps the studio in which he most likely learned his trade was Fra Angelico's.

The eight pictures which were once between the pilasters and over the *predella*, all larger but on a variety of scales, are of course by Piero's own hand. They were evidently arranged in two tiers, with the centre picture of each tier, which is larger than those on either side, rising above the rest. The plinth which forms the base for the group in the large centre panel is continued into the two shorter panels on either side, where the pairs of Saints stand barefoot on the bare stone. Between this centre panel and those on either side of it there was evidently a carved and gilt pilaster or, more likely, a self-supporting pillaret; but behind each of these the extremities of a kneeling devotee are extended from under the Virgin's mantle into the next picture with its two Saints standing side by side. Above *The Virgin of Mercy* was *The Crucifixion*, with the Virgin and St John Evangelist crying aloud at the foot of the Cross. Two of the pictures on either side of this form an *Annunciation*; the other two have each a standing *Saint*.

The frame of the altarpiece must have tied all these pictures together by the rhythm of the five round arches in its main tier, dominated by the largest in the centre; and Piero evidently did his best to create between this gilded arcade and the gilded backgrounds a sense of space in which the Saints had equal rights to light and air with the Virgin and her protégés. Nevertheless the ensemble could be called old-fashioned in comparison with those altarpieces already painted in Florence in which the Saints and Donors are gathered round the Madonna in a single spacious scene. Its form may have been due, as is usually suggested, to the insistence of a conservative provincial confraternity; but the same explanation then has to be given for the polyptych form of at least two altarpieces painted considerably later in Piero's career. In the meantime, he was as yet undeveloped as a painter and may well have been glad to find his way slowly, almost from figure to figure. Artists, and the profound, original artists no more than the rest, cannot immediately use to the full the large ideas that they admire in the work of others, so that there is perhaps no evidence about the length of his stay in Florence in the fact that this altarpiece yields no sign that Piero had seen any of these pictures there. What it does show, more significantly, is that he had gone, so to speak, behind Angelico and Domenico, to the source of light, fully grasping Masaccio's principle of illumination. Unless – as is not impossible – he was already in Florence as a boy some twenty years before, it would seem that he must have gone to Pisa to see Masaccio's polyptych there, of which the central *Madonna* is now in the National Gallery, London, and *The Crucifixion* at Capodimonte, Naples.

It is by no means easy to appreciate to the full the remains of this first altarpiece by Piero without the frame; for this not only held all the eight pictures together but provided for each of them a base to support forms of weight and power. The illusion is considerably frustrated now by the appearance, for instance, of several inches of unpainted panel beneath the plinth, in the pictures, on which all the figures of the main tier stand or kneel. One has to hold up a book and exclude these ragged lower ends from one's own vision in order to regain from the pictures above them that sense of weight and third dimension which is the very essence of Piero's art. Yet, in spite of this untidy levitation and of the diversity of their scale, these twenty figures remain united by the consistency of the light in which Piero has revealed them to us. Coming from above on our right, it is reflected most clearly in the eyes of the ecstatic upturned faces, those of the little band under the Virgin's cloak, of the naked *St Sebastian* on the left of the main tier. This is certainly the first nude by Piero to survive, seeming clumsy and little observed in comparison with the convincing figures which are to follow within a few years. Yet even the clumsiness and the over-simplified contours are those of a man with a grasp of form. There is strength in the bold sweep of the outlines, and it is substance in which the arrows are embedded, flesh which presses outwards from the inside with the principle of growth. Standing so firmly on its marble plinth, this figure has a weight like that of few other figures painted since Masaccio had died. Nothing is so typical of the genius of Masaccio and of Piero as this simple fact. Giotto's figures stand like this, but not those of even the greatest of the Gothic painters. It is not so much the result of a technical effort as of an attitude of mind.

Throughout the whole group of pictures, in spite of archaic gilded backgrounds scarcely to be seen again in Piero's work, the illusion of the third dimension is powerful. In the centre panel one can almost feel the heaviness of the Virgin's fur-lined mantle, put one's fingers into the reflected light within its folds, breathe the warmed air which envelops the eager little mortals gathered into it. On either side, the deep folds of the raiment of the Saints harbour shadows of which the colour is intensified by its own reflections, especially in the case of the different reds of the mantles of the two Saints who stand nearest to the Madonna, *St John Baptist* on the left, *St Andrew* on the right. *St Bernardino*, the ascetic monk on the extreme right, has a habit of monochrome grey, toning with the curiously grey body of St Sebastian on the other side; and it must have been above these two that Piero placed the two little monastic Saints in their monochrome habits, *St Benedict* in off-white over St Sebastian, *St Francis* in warm grey over St Bernardino. Thus the glowing colour was concentrated towards the centre of the altarpiece.

While the lighting, the strong modelling of the forms and the depth of the colour in the main tier are inspired by the general principles of Masaccio, it is in the *Crucifixion* above that one recognises the particular stimulus of one of his compositions. Piero had evidently seen Masaccio's *Crucifixion* which is now at Naples. In Piero's picture the figures have perhaps even more weight than in Masaccio's; but then Masaccio had gone out of his way to make his St John an almost girlish figure in order to express the forlornness of the youngest disciple at the loss of a master upon whom he had depended. He is huddled into himself in full realisation of the finality of the scene. Piero's Evangelist has just arrived upon it. The terrible realisation that the soul has gone from the body is expressed in a traditional gesture of arms flung wide apart, in dramatic contrast with the Virgin, whose two hands are outstretched in profile before her in an agony of prayer. Only in the sleeves does one see the crimson of the Virgin's robe. Everything else is covered by her great black mantle, of which it is hard at first to discern more than the starkly sculptured outline of its bulk; but the folds are there, more nobly modelled than those of any of the figures of the main tier. St John's brilliant blue robe is almost covered by his loose mantle of bright rose, and in this one can see more easily that the design of the folds is infinitely more masterly than anything below. Indeed, if one looks across to the rose mantle of the life-size Christ in Piero's fresco of *The Resurrection* in the same room, it is difficult to say that in this mature masterpiece the design of the mantle is stronger or more beautiful; it is only better controlled, more concisely described. Piero's *Crucifixion*, like Masaccio's, is designed to be looked at from below as the physical climax of his altarpiece; and it is the climax also in expression.

Yet in this series of eight pictures it is not perhaps the most advanced. To the right side of *The Crucifixion*, the *Madonna of the Annunciation* has become a rather faint and flattened image owing to a technical characteristic which has had a similar effect on the other little panel, with *St Francis*, on the same side and on the wide panel below with *SS. Andrew and Bernardino*. The ground of white gesso, a mixture of gypsum and glue, with which all the panels were covered before Piero began to paint, has on this side of the altarpiece broken into a particularly coarse network of deep and wide cracks. On the other side, however, the craquelure is normal; so that in the little *Annunciation* panel with the figure of the *Archangel Gabriel* one can still enjoy the full power of the effect. And indeed this is perhaps literally the most brilliant colour that any painter had yet achieved. In the pictures of the main tier the effect of light is warm and rather muted. *The Crucifixion* above it is considerably more luminous; but it can perhaps still be questioned whether this wonderful light is that of the sun. With Gabriel, however, there is no question; he has brought down with him from heaven the blazing light of the sky. The fillet on his head, the girdle at his waist and his stocking-slippers are of scarlet; the great mass of colour in his long tunic is a pale lavender blue, which in its deep shadows changes to a warm lilac mauve. With the scarlet as its foil, this impalpable colour seems to sing aloud. Not even Fra Angelico achieved a more heavenly effect. One does not know whether to describe it as colour or as light. Piero has made them the same.

There is no record of the delivery of the altarpiece. In 1462, seventeen years after the signing of the contract promising delivery in three years, Piero's brother Marco received on his behalf from the same confraternity 'fifteen *scudi* as part payment for the picture which his brother M. Pietro has painted'; and from this entry in an account book concerning a picture which cannot be identified it has been deduced that Piero had lingered all these years over the painting of the eight pictures. If the reference is indeed to the altarpiece, there is always the possibility that it was the members of the Confraternity who had been in arrears, no less scandalously, with payment for a picture which had been finished long ago. It seems unlikely that Piero himself would have behaved so casually – and in his home town – over the execution of what, as far as we know, was the first important commission that he received. It is also difficult to explain the more developed character of the pictures that followed if his ideas and his method did not evolve considerably while he was working on this group.

It is another thing to point out that St Bernardino was not canonised until 1450, a mere five years after the contract was signed; but the fact that Piero has included him and has equipped him with a halo is anything but conclusive evidence that the painter was even two years late in completing his task. Here one has only to look at his halo and that of St Andrew beside him, polished discs drawn in true perspective which reflect the tops of the two bald heads, to see that this panel is indeed a little more mature than that with SS. Sebastian and John Baptist on the other side, but seventeen years are not necessary for such a development. Piero himself may have met Bernardino, and in any case the future Saint would have been seen in the flesh by many visitors to the Chapel of the Misericordia; and this accounts for the fact that, unlike the other Saints, he seems to be portrayed from the life. But this by no means makes him the most satisfying figure of the altarpiece. *The Crucifixion* is a much more beautiful picture, and certainly no less developed, and it is still recording the direct impact upon Piero of Masaccio's ideas. There is no other picture with characteristics which suggest that it was painted in an interval between one panel and another of this altarpiece, and therefore there is little reason to suggest that Piero did not carry out his promise in time.

Perhaps more than that of any other painter, the art of Piero della Francesca can be seen from his pictures to have evolved less in the course of his experience at the easel or on the wall-face – protracted though this was – than between his successive pictures, by the process of thought. One of the fascinating things about the series from this altarpiece is that in it Piero has already established for ever both the strongly marked character of his forms and his manner of describing them. His St Sebastian may be cruder than any of his subsequent nudes, but even he has the sturdy, functional feet and ankles which Piero will give to all his male figures in the pictures to come, modelled always in much the same way. Even from St Sebastian's immature head the rudiments of Piero's characteristic method of representing hair are already sprouting – a few tough and wiry strands standing out from a generalised mass of colour, as befits his broad simplification of form. Piero's hands, while they are wonderfully expressive, are like his feet, always retaining the qualities already to be found throughout his altarpiece. They are practical, peasant hands, with square palms, weighty knuckles and strong, short fingers. They are suitable for his men and women, who are themselves unchanging. Their gestures are of the simplest. They stand firmly here at the beginning looking straight before them, and they are still standing there firmly at the end of Piero's painting career with the same unwavering expression. It is mostly the atmosphere and the space around them that have changed.

THE POLYPTYCH OF THE MISERICORDIA
Palazzo Comunale, Sansepolcro

V

VII

VIII   IX

XII

5 · Early Development

V - XIV
23

The *Misericordia* altarpiece, unlikely as it is to have been Piero's very first effort, remains the earliest evidence of how congenital was his sense of volume and of space and atmosphere.* The next dated picture, the fresco at Rimini of 1451, shows with what extraordinary rapidity he welded these qualities into a harmonious instrument of expression, but also that he must have painted other pictures in the interval.

50

Plainly intermediate is the small altarpiece *The Madonna and Child with four Angels* in the Sterling and Francine Clark Institute at Williamstown, Mass. The Angels are reminiscent of the Saints in the polyptych, and indeed the two standing in front, who might well be the same Angel seen in profile and three-quarter view, have already appeared there as the Archangel of the Annunciation. For all the simplicity of her dress, the *Madonna della Misericordia* is sister to the enthroned Virgin of Domenico Veneziano in Bucharest, with her forehead shaved far back like those of ladies in the height of fashion. This Madonna comes almost straight from the farm. She holds out the flower in her hand with an arm which has been carved in that position. She has the massive strength of mountains. The group as a whole has so much weight that it seemed uncomfortably out of place when I last saw it, in a frame which has no plinth at its foot, hung in line with other pictures, but out of centre. To be appreciated, it had to be detached and stood upon the floor. The stiffness and clumsiness which perhaps inevitably characterise monumentality in its beginnings and which may well have been what inhibited Piero from himself attempting the small scale of the *predella* and pilaster figures of the polyptych, are much in evidence when the Clark altarpiece is reproduced in black and white. They are dissolved by the airiness of its colour and light. Nor does this brilliance allow one to notice the immaturity of the composition itself, the fact that, if this stony figure were to become bone and flesh and to stand upright, she would make a doll's house of the little cloister in which she is enthroned. Alberti, the great aesthete of the century, had already in his treatise *On Painting* criticised pictures 'in which a man is placed in a building as in a closed casket where there is scarcely room to sit down'. With Masaccio's frescoes no doubt in mind, he had continued 'all bodies should harmonise in size and function with what is happening in the history'. Perhaps Alberti's is the first use of the word *historia* which led to the term 'history-painting', a phrase to enter common parlance later on for any composition which involves some degree of movement or action. He can hardly have been thinking of the votive Madonna which was still the subject most demanded of the painter; or he might well have made allowance for such a dilemma as confronted Piero here: how to reconcile the demand of the conventional patron, or patrons, for a Virgin who occupies most of the picture space with his own wish to create such an illusion as Alberti advocated of space in which the figures seem free to circulate.

* For a *Madonna* considered by Longhi and others to be an early work by Piero, see 20.

Just as many of the types of men and women which Piero uses all his life are established in the earliest pictures, so it is with the motifs of his architecture. These elegant fluted columns with Corinthian capitals supporting a richly carved entablature, all in white stone but enclosing panels of dark, richly coloured marble, are to be found henceforward at intervals in his work with little variation. What will mostly change is the relationship to the figures. Here it might seem that the whole composition was carved out of one piece of stone were it not for the singing quality of the colour, which is bound up with the vitality of the light. Piero's supreme gift for colour is already revealed in essence. In contrast with Masaccio's, his hues are predominantly cool. Yet in comparison with Angelico's, they seem to be organic and inseparable from his sense of eternal form. It would be absurd to suggest that he needed any instruction, even if any other case were known of a great artist doing what a critic told him. Yet the kind of harmony which he here achieved had already been in part described by Alberti, prophetically and far more poetically than I can do in a description of this picture: 'There is a certain friendship of colours, so that one joined with another gives dignity and grace. Rose near to green and to sky blue gives both honour and life. White, not only near to ash and to crocus yellow but placed beside almost any other colour, gives gladness. Dark colours stand among light with dignity, and the light colours turn about among the dark.' While the Virgin in the centre of this picture is clad in the traditional ultramarine mantle over the traditional robe of crimson, patterned here with gold, it happens that the rose-crimson tunic of the Angel on the right is seen between his own emerald wings and the deeper green tunic of the Angel next to him, who has wings of sky blue. On the other side the colour is cooler and lighter, with one of the two Angels in white, the other in blue-grey with blue-green shadows; there are blue-grey wings for the white tunic, and for the blue-grey tunic wings of brilliant rose, which reaches extraordinary intensity in the deep shadow where it is glimpsed under the Angel's arm.

This distribution of the colours reinforces the effect of light flooding in from the left. It is brilliant as the light of Angelico, but it has a greater significance in its sharper contrasts and because of its greater involvement with the forms. We forget any crudities which these may have in the magic of the illusion of light, which is all one with the colour and the form. A new acuteness of observation has discovered new fields of beauty, above all in the areas of reflected light. As beautiful as any of the colours, and making a cool foil for their variety and sunlit warmth, is the white face of the upper step to the Virgin's throne. It is all in shadow, and this falls so tenderly into the shallow carving of the rosettes that one marvels at the sheer beauty of light and feels convinced that the form was there before the light, to give it meaning. Across the step below, with its upper surface reflecting the full light, falls the shadow of a column. This unseen column can only be the pair of the one that faces us from behind the Virgin's back; and thus the illusion of space is complete. 'Know,' Alberti had written, 'that a painted thing can never appear truthful where there is not a definite distance for seeing it.'

Leon Battista degli Alberti was the first of those men of universal genius who seem characteristic of the Renaissance. Interested in everything, he was prepared to write on almost any subject. After studying the law, civil and canon, he had obtained an appointment to the Papal Curia in 1431, and had perhaps in these early

years in Rome begun upon his *Descriptio urbis Romae*, not to mention some amateur
painting at which he seems to hint, or at least some experiments with pictorial
perspective. In the train of the virtually exiled Eugenius IV he came in 1434 to
Florence; was filled immediately with enthusiasm for the works of Brunelleschi
and Donatello and Masaccio; and stayed to become the propagandist of the new
movement. His treatise on painting was written in Latin – *De Pictura* – in 1435. He
himself translated it into Italian – *Della Pittura* – the following year.* This book,
already quoted in relation to the Clark altarpiece, is the first on the theory of
painting. Superficially, it is given an antique air today by the numerous citations
from Greek and Latin authors and by the recommendation of themes from ancient
history and mythology. But even these could have seemed appropriate and valid
well into the nineteenth century and, when Alberti wrote, such themes had still to
be painted for the first time since Antiquity. In their day these very recommenda-
tions were revolutionary. Their adoption was to be a landmark in the history of
painting. Alberti's mathematical method of perspective construction and the reticu-
lated veil which he advocated to relate objects in space and relocate them in the
illusion of space to be created have been superseded by simpler methods; but his is
the first written theory of perspective. It is the intention that counts, and the
research into mathematics as the base of all knowledge is itself characteristic of his
intention. His book is concerned with the fundamentals of vision and of visual
experience, and it remains a brief and vivid exposition of what Masaccio and many
of the great painters who followed in his footsteps aimed to do. Artists in the
twentieth century have gradually turned their backs upon nature. To the painters
of the Renaissance nature meant man himself and all the visible world surrounding
him, and their purpose was to master nature by recreating her within the four sides
of a frame. By reason of the mere selectivity, not to mention the skills, required
this was a tremendous task, mentally as well as technically. In the language of
words Alberti gives a unique glimpse into the mind of the Renaissance artist,
not only because he understood what had been achieved by Masaccio, the only
painter whom he mentions in a prologue virtually dedicating his Italian edition to
Brunelleschi, but because from 1436, when he completed this, it almost certainly,
however unlikely this seems, gave inspiration and often instruction to ambitious
painters. Alberti's opportunity was a rare one. Though a generation younger than
Brunelleschi, he was in almost at the birth of the greatest artistic movement since
Greek times. He had the genius to appreciate the opportunity, and his reward was
possibly a unique position in history as a critic who played a constructive part in
forwarding a revolution. He did this first as a writer and then as an architect.

On his return to Rome, he had not only plunged again into the study of ancient
architecture but had become the practical adviser to Pope Nicholas V in restoring
some outstanding monuments and in giving the city a new plan. Meanwhile he
began to design great buildings outside Rome. It was in what was perhaps the first
of these, the cathedral at Rimini, on the Adriatic coast, that Piero painted what is
probably the first fresco of his to survive, though it is unlikely to have been by any
means his earliest exercise in the medium. This is *Sigismondo Malatesta kneeling to*
St Sigismund, painted in the cathedral's Chapel of the Relics. Piero himself, or an
assistant, must have written the inscriptions along the base in bold Roman letters

* John R. Spencer, *Alberti: On Painting*, 1956; English translation with a valuable introduction and notes.

which identify the subject, the artist and the date. This is thus the fourth document which we have concerning him. The dedication . SANCTVS SIGISMVNDVS . SIGISMVNDVS PANDVLFVS MALATESTA . PAN F is followed in letters half the size by PETRI DE BVRGO O[PVS] / MCCCCLI .

Piero has crossed the Apennines and, as we know from a first glance at this fresco, has grown in stature during the few years between. In the *Misericordia* triptych the incipient grandeur was more in the expression than in the design, and in the Clark altarpiece the design is still immature. The immediately striking feature of this fresco is the spacious, decorative, entirely classical framework of architecture within which Piero has set the two figures of Sigismondo and his patron saint. Scarcely less striking to a contemporary must have been the treatment of the subject. Portraiture had been introduced into religious compositions for centuries, and Masaccio, Domenico Veneziano, even Angelico had introduced contemporaries in other characters than those of donor or of devotee. But here it is Malatesta who is the real subject of the picture. He takes the centre. He and his dogs and a miniature of his recently built stronghold occupy most of the picture space. No doubt he dictated his requirements to the painter, substituting for the universally worshipped Madonna a little known Burgundian saint of the sixth century who had the good fortune to be a patron to a Malatesta. But it was Piero presumably who devised the clever scheme by which the nominal subject of the picture is relegated to a secondary position in it without unseemliness and the tyrant is presented in the centre almost like a Roman conqueror, under great swags of laurel.

This wide architrave of pale stone, with exquisite classical ornament appearing to be chiselled in low relief, is no mere painted frame; it is an essential part of the composition. It provides a kind of open façade to a recess of the same height, though it is much wider, as we know from the curve of the laurel swags on the wall behind, disappearing on either side behind the architrave. The walls and floor of this recess are – or rather were – faced with rich, dark marble in panels surrounded by the same stone. On the floor bands of stone run inward from the base of the architrave to an imaginary vanishing-point behind Malatesta, actually to end inside the bases of the two fluted pilasters which divide the wall behind. These with their Corinthian capitals support a frieze of stone which is parallel to and level with the architrave in front. The fresco has been detached from the wall on which it was painted; but the amount of this frieze which is visible through the architrave, together with the foreshortened pavement below, still tells us the height at which the picture should be seen, given the distance at which we can most easily view the composition as a whole.

If there is a weakness in the logic of the design, it is that the measurable width established by the curve of the swag for the partly seen marble panel on the right is difficult to reconcile with the position of the round stone frame set into it. Through this we have a telescopic view of the citadel which Malatesta had constructed in Rimini a few years before, as is proudly recorded by the inscription carved on it: CASTELLVM SISMVNDVM . ARIMINENSE MCCCCXLVI. Over the castle roofs the sky is blue, and we are left free to wonder whether this should seem an actual view through an embrasure in the wall or a carving in low relief with a coloured ground.

If this is indeed a flaw in the design, it has become much exaggerated by the appearance of the picture since it was restored at some date before 1954. The effect of the whole has been much damaged, though for the most part the painting is not in bad state. The parts where modelling was required are unequally preserved; but the heads and hands appear to be in fair condition, together with everything that is painted without colour: the lining of St Sigismund's mantle, the two greyhounds and all the architecture except the marbles of the background. It is in these large areas, and especially in the widest in the centre, that the damage is more serious, and it is here that it could have been repaired without great difficulty if the restorer, who removed a spurious skyscape which had been painted over them in 1820, had not reacted to this impiety by leaving only the distracting confusion of a ruined surface. With its restlessness and its light, warm tone, this background has become atmospherically a foreground to most of the painting, bringing the well-preserved light parts, including the roundel, forward with it. The illusion of depth is thus almost lost. Once it was considerable. The background wall seems now to be close against the further side of the dais; but this dais is at a distance from us, as we know from the foreshortening of the bands of pale stone in the floor, and it is a substantial affair, with a step up to it under the heavy carpet and room on it to take the draped throne of St Sigismund, which is set diagonally. The saint was King of Burgundy for a year, retiring in remorse to a monastery when he discovered that he had wrongly condemned his own son to death; and he sits there royally under his halo and his large hat, orb and sceptre in hand, listening to the prayer of his namesake, and wondering perhaps at the presence of Sigismondo's two enormous dogs. His grave, substantial figure is bathed in sympathetic light, which fills the space around him. Indeed, if one has recourse once more to holding up a book, this time to cover the whole centre with Malatesta, which is the part worst damaged, one can still recover a great sense of depth on either side. The architrave must once have framed a splendid space. Though what lay beyond the architrave is not all to be seen now, the outlines are all there, to show that the design was measured and symmetrical; and the diagonal presentation of the figures is rhythmical and deeply impressive in the slow music of its spacing.

The quite uneven preservation of different parts of the picture suggests that the method of painting was not uniform, that the marbles of the background and some parts of the costumes were not painted in true fresco. In this fresco technique the colours, mixed with water as a medium, have to be applied to the plaster while it is wet so that, as the plaster dries and re-crystallises, the pigment particles may be locked among the crystals. The colours thus become an integral part of the wall's surface, to endure as long as it endures. Before the painting is begun, to make sure that it fits correctly in the allotted space, the composition has to be drawn complete on a first layer of plaster; and this has to be coated again with new plaster, applied section by section so that it can be painted in colour while this plaster is wet. Painters of all periods were often content to do only the figures, or even only the heads, in true fresco, painting the rest on the dried plaster, usually in the egg tempera medium. Colour which is not incorporated in the plaster scales off inevitably with time. Piero could hardly have expected that, when the day came for repairs, as it must do with all pictures, there would be conscientious objections – as there presumably have been here – to the reconstruction of a merely decorative background.

He may on this occasion have been given insufficient time. His patron was in many ways a notoriously impatient man, not perhaps without reason. Those who valued the lives of others as cheaply as did Malatesta carried their own in their hands. Yet the precariousness of life in those days only seems to have incited men to set about the raising of great monuments that would endure, and their embellishment with detail of every kind which required an infinity of labour in its execution. The typical despot was not happy without the sound of stonemasons and sculptors working to materialise his glory in permanent and wonderful form.

The fresco does not provide proof that Sigismondo, the son of Pandolfo Malatesta, actually sat to Piero della Francesca. The profile portrait and the view of the Malatesta citadel could both have been adapted from the low reliefs which the sculptor Matteo dei Pasti had already made in bronze. Nevertheless, the two men are likely to have been in contact, for it pleased Sigismondo to converse with intelligent men, especially if they were prepared to help perpetuate his name.

He provides an example of the extraordinary contrasts which made up the character and the fortunes of many famous men of the Italian Renaissance who ruled so precariously over the petty states. At this time he had managed to be lord of Rimini already for twenty years, but his fortunes were beginning to decline and he was barely in possession when he died after another seventeen. Men in his position had to keep their own subjects disarmed and hire mercenary soldiers from elsewhere. Their best hope of surviving and of keeping their coffers full was to become *condottieri*, commanders of an army of mercenaries which they hired out with themselves to the great powers like Venice and Milan, the Papacy and the Kingdom of Naples. Each of these Sigismondo served in turn, and in turn came to be distrusted and detested for his perfidy and utter lack of scruple. His dominions were declared forfeit to the Holy See by Pius II, who had him burned in effigy as 'king of traitors, the enemy of God and man'. Yet Pius, who was a great scholar, felt obliged to acknowledge publicly the other side of his character. 'Sigismondo knew antiquity, and had a great store of philosophy,' he noted in his *Commentaries*.

Rimini had been a town of some importance in Roman times. A bridge begun by the Emperor Augustus and finished by Tiberius is still in use; the triumphal arch of Augustus is still standing, and there are remains of a Roman amphitheatre. Sigismondo made it for a moment a centre of the revival of Antiquity. He imported the relics not of a saint but of a Greek philosopher and had a series of sarcophagi made for his ashes and those of the contemporary scholars and humanists whom he attracted to his court. These used to meet and hold discussions in the new citadel depicted by Piero, sitting under their '*rex*', where they sang his praises and those of his beloved Isotta in Latin verse.

With such aids alone Sigismondo might have remained only a figure in local history or a name quoted by specialists as a splendid example of a type. What has perpetuated the more than half pagan glory of himself and his Isotta, thereby fulfilling the main ambition of his life, is the building which Piero thus helped to decorate with yet another of the tyrant's effigies. Rimini cathedral was originally S. Francesco, a great barn built in austerely simple Gothic to hold the swollen congregations of the preaching friars. Since Sigismondo's day it has been known more suitably as the '*Tempio Malatestiano*', the 'Malatesta Temple'. The cipher which crops up all over the interior, wherever it can best be seen, is not the holy *IHS* but

IS or *SI*, for Sigismondo and Isotta. Under the direction of Matteo dei Pasti the spare Gothic piers were encased in Renaissance columns standing in sculptured baskets from which the squeezed fruit overflows in bronze. The walls were encrusted with reliefs of fascinating girls who represent the Arts and the Sciences, and provocative little Loves abound poorly disguised as budding Angels in the enchanting reliefs of Agostino di Duccio.

Outside, the flanks of the Gothic church have been buried deep behind two colossal single-storey arcades, one of them sheltering a series of austere sarcophagi for the bones of humanists. The front, screened with three arches inspired perhaps by the neighbouring triumphal arch of Augustus, has become the most thoroughly classical façade of the fifteenth century. Standing before this great building, still unfinished, one could easily believe that it is by Palladio, the architect whose name has provided an adjective for the measured simplicities of the fully classical style of the next century. In fact it was designed by Alberti.

It can by no means be assumed that Piero and Alberti were actually together in Rimini, for an inscription on the façade of the *Tempio* shows that the building was well advanced in 1450, and Alberti notoriously liked to execute his architecture by sending detailed instructions to the stonemasons from Rome. But two such seekers after the truth may well in their progress have sought each other's company. One can hardly credit Piero with any of the architect's unusual fondness for using richly coloured materials, for Alberti's book on painting proves that he had long had a painter's eye for it, and it seems to follow naturally from his way of thinking as an architect, equally unusual at this date, in mass rather than in line. On the other hand, a great leap forward in Piero's composition, a sudden attainment to his full grandeur and spaciousness, have to be accounted for; and it is legitimate perhaps to wonder whether Alberti could have drawn the plan for Piero's fresco. It provides a beautiful illustration of the premises from which he starts in the *Della pittura* on his exposition of artificial perspective. In Piero's fresco, more clearly and emphatically than in any picture yet painted, and by means which are essentially architectural, the picture plane is established by the painted architrave, 'the open window', as Alberti wrote, 'through which I see what is to be painted there'. The foreshortened pavement beyond it is the measured base of the cubic space depicted, and this space was created clearly before the forms which came to inhabit it. In the symmetry with which it is divided one scents a theory of architectural proportion in a simple and grand form, and the architecture has all the features of Alberti's design: the flatness of the surfaces, the wide intervals in the generous breadth, the pale features contrasted with fields of deep, rich colour. In his books on sculpture and architecture there is stress on the musical relationship of proportions. Perhaps it was Alberti's music which inspired the simple, emphatic spacing of the fresco.

Its main theme is brought into the open air in a little panel picture which has been since 1850 in the Accademia in Venice: *Gerolamo Amadi kneeling to St Jerome*. The Saint's crucifix is fixed in the sawn-off bole of a tree, and on this natural pedestal Piero has carved: PETRI DE BV̄ / GO S̄CI SEP/VLCRI OPVS. A probably different and rather later hand has identified the devotee by writing below his effigy: HIER AMADI AVG. F. It would be easy to believe that this Gerolamo, or Jerome, son of an Augustus, if he did not actually come from Rimini, had at least seen Piero's picture there of Malatesta kneeling to St Sigismund, and had asked him to repeat the idea in a fashion modestly befitting an Amadi. The family has not been traced; but at least they are unlikely to have been of Sansepolcro. Piero would probably not have signed his name in this way if he had been painting for a fellow-citizen in their birthplace; nor does this little town at the foot of the hills appear to be Sansepolcro. According to Longhi* no less than thirty-five domestic chimney pots are to be counted in it, all of a design peculiar to the Veneto. We know nothing of Piero going any nearer to Venice than Ferrara, where it is unlikely that such an architectural rule applied; but from Ferrara, where he undoubtedly worked, to Venice itself is a comparatively short journey, which could be made in comfort by boat; and it is hard to believe that Piero ever got so near to the fabulous city without going through a part of the Veneto to see it.

However, this is a landscape, and probably the first real landscape which we have from Piero's hand. Though the paint is very little damaged otherwise, the appearance of the scene has been greatly altered by the darkening of all the greens. Originally they must have been a brilliant contrast with St Jerome's white shift and the rich, soft wine colour of Gerolamo's gown, deeply pleated and enormous in the sleeves. In paintings of the fourteenth and fifteenth centuries the majority of the greens were made from a pigment prepared as verdigris, which is best ground in resin rather than in oil. Brilliant greens result; but, as this paint oxidises under the influence of light, it gradually turns brown, even almost black, as probably in the carpet under the *Madonna della Misericordia*. Yet this drastic change of colour and a general coating of varnish gone brown have altered surprisingly little the quite new naturalness of this scene. The composition seems to be the result of instinct rather than of design, and it would seem that Piero has trusted in nature to provide the unity. Artificiality would have spoiled the convincing attitude of the old Church Father, his body spare with fastings, his gaze straightforward and penetrating as he hears his namesake's confession. This is a deeply religious picture conceived in humanist terms. There is nothing remote in the relationship between the earnest burgher and his intermediary with God, and both are at one with nature in the beautiful god-given Italian light. Again, as with his architecture, the character of Piero's landscape scarcely changes, though he soon had opportunities to develop it on a bigger scale.

Of his work at Ferrara not a trace remains. There is therefore no certainty of the date at which he painted either the frescoes in a chapel of the long ago demolished church of S. Agostino there, which are mentioned by Vasari as already suffering from the damp, or those in the old palace of the Este, which was to be torn down and reconstructed almost within a generation of their execution. But there is a good deal of evidence that Piero was at Ferrara by 1449, two years before he painted the fresco at Rimini, and at least the frescoes in the palace are likely to have been painted for Lionello d'Este in the last year or two of his reign. At Ferrara the Este had a more secure base for their power than did the Malatesta at Rimini. Under their more peaceful and more genuinely sophisticated rule the city became a great centre in the fifteenth century and the early sixteenth, the university a fountain source of humanism, the court a lively and luxurious exhibition of the arts, especially that of the theatre. At Ferrara, more probably indeed than at Rimini,

*Longhi, *op. cit.*, pp. 201–2.

Piero may have met and had discussions with Alberti, who was patronised by both Lionello and his brother Meliaduso and dedicated books to them.

Perhaps some copies of the frescoes in the palace were made before they were destroyed, and perhaps these found an echo in two sixteenth-century pictures in oil on panel, one in the Walters Collection at Baltimore, the other in the National Gallery, London. Restless, over-dramatised compositions, with figures wearing the costumes of about 1530, these nevertheless have some features plainly borrowed more or less directly from Piero della Francesca, including a remarkable luminosity. Since the hand appears to be Ferrarese, it may well be to Piero's frescoes at Ferrara that these panels are indebted. *

They share a very effective use of white horses with a little picture by Piero's own hand which may be a more reliable key to the character of the Este frescoes. 63 This is the little *Crucifixion* bequeathed by Mrs John D. Rockefeller II to the Frick Collection, New York. One has to give many minutes to this picture before one can enjoy it as it deserves, for the years have not been kind to it. Much of the finished surface is badly worn and there has been some retouching. With the forms thus weakened, the whole composition is more affected than it might have been by the heavy, irregular network of deep cracks which makes a rival pattern and often interferes with the lines of the composition. Instead of sky, there is a background of gold, and the horizon is now almost lost among the irrelevant and coarser lines of the craquelure. Between this and the figures the landscape is largely rubbed away, and among the *dramatis personae* only the horses are wholly unimpaired. Alternately roan and white, they are sturdy and vigorous as the horses on antique coins. Yet the effect of light is still largely there throughout. Under the three banners, deep scarlet, geranium pink and grey-mauve against the gold sky, the figures still preserve the masses of their clear, bright colour. St John, again, rebels against the facts, his garment crying out with its brilliant rose to sustain the agony of his movement. Between him and the fainting Virgin on the other side of the Cross, the three soldiers seated round the confiscated robe at the very foot are completely detached in their own greedy interests. With a studied gesture one of them picks the first straw from the three held out by a companion, while the third man is absorbed in the lottery's result. They are grouped with extraordinary skill, these three, naturally and yet performing an essential function in the monumental design. The right leg of the man choosing his straw is in a direct line with the upright of the Cross, so that the composition is cleft in two from top to bottom down the very centre, the cleavage between the two wedge-shaped groups leaving significant space for the Cross and expressing the lonely agony of its burden. Yet round its base the three together form a chain which binds the two groups together in the space. And space there is. To enlarge this scene to any size would be to make it only proportionately more impressive in its grandeur.

Piero must then have gone back home over the Apennines to paint another altarpiece, *The Baptism of Christ*, now in the National Gallery, London. The largest 22 single panel which we have from his hand until we reach the very end of his career, this was almost certainly the high altarpiece of the church of the Priory of S. Giovanni Battista at Sansepolcro, though its history is a little confused, and no contemporary record has been brought to light. Sansepolcro appears in it, tiny

* The National Gallery picture is No. 1062. See Martin Davies, *The Early Italian Schools*, pp. 434-5.

with distance, remote, as befits the sacramental theme, but conspicuous in the bright light under the very elbow of Christ, with its white road at an angle which draws the beholder's eye. So the scene is brought within the compass of his own experience, even while the smallness of his town gives grandeur and immediacy to the five figures ranged in line across the foreground.

Again, but this time on a considerable scale and this time with greens which have darkened less than those in Gerolamo Amadi's little picture, the landscape is constructed with a naturalness which is something quite new in the history of painting. Piero does not like vagueness, but nor does he attempt to create form where form could not be discerned. In the background these little copses and clumps of trees and patches of scrub which interrupt with their wayward patterns the smooth green and grey of grass and soil are blobbed on in a manner which must have seemed quite unprofessional to Piero's critics; but somehow they leave no doubt about the shape and substance of the limestone hills they clothe. In the foreground the little plants are not formal and semi-heraldic like those of Angelico, but nor are they organic or rooted in the soil; they are like flowers stuck by some child into his temporary garden of sand, and seem to be only space-fillers and distance-markers, as are the rather irritating little clouds which float above the scene. Yet one can almost breathe the upland air, can almost set one's foot on the road to Sansepolcro. The two main figures seem to have been blocked in first, at least in outline, before Piero began to paint the landscape; but that is all. Like Malatesta's noble side-lit hall at Rimini, this outdoor space seems to have been created first; or, if not, the three Angels and the lesser subsidiary figures were altered considerably before he finished them. This much we know from the increased transparency of the paint, which now allows the landscape to be visible through parts of all but the two main figures. The picture is painted throughout in pure tempera, in a technique which had been traditional in Italy for two centuries. Unlike Sassetta, whose great polyptych had been set in place on the high altar of S. Francesco at Sansepolcro in June 1444, Piero mixed his paint almost as thin as watercolour; so that in the flesh the underpainting in *terra verde* shows more than usual through the thin over-painting of the shadows, to make these especially clear and translucent in contrast with the warm, white, opaque overpainting in the parts which take the full light. Even Angelico's bodies are not so brilliant as these. This proof that the majority of the figures either were put in after the landscape had been painted or were drastically altered as Piero continued to create until the picture was finished may dispose of the idea that he allowed any definite geometric system to dictate the composition; but the spontaneity can only enhance the grandeur of his thoughtfully considered three-dimensional design.

The high altar is always placed on the axial line of the church; so that this imaginary line upon which the symmetry of the building is ordered must have led the eye straight to the figure of Christ standing in the very centre, and up it to the baptismal cup and the hovering Dove representing the Holy Spirit, to end in the centre of the arch overhead. An arch to the frame has a special value when it closes a vista in this way; and Piero has made full use of the implied circle in the construction of the scene. Our eye is inclined to complete it below, and the left arm of the Baptist, the top of Christ's loincloth are found to lie more or less along the unseen line of its circumference. The snowy Dove hovers on it equidistant from the two sides. On a line with the horizontal shoulders of the panel, it suggests the division of its height in the ratio 2:3, just as the nearest tree by the clear outline along its right side seems to make the same division of the width. While these potential measurements give proportion to the surface plan, the impression of a third dimension is made inescapable by a kind of rough geometry in the many curves which seem to echo that of the arch: the spread of the trees above, the hollow of the hills rising behind, the meandering of the Jordan river transplanted into Umbria, the many sharper curves of smaller or more distant things. The movement of all these is inward and outward as well as up and down, giving depth and height to the space of Piero's creation. The leaves of the tree are arched forward to the very front of this space, to the plane of the picture's frame, setting Christ's head well back within it, as the ground before him does with his feet. Thus the landscape becomes a great bowl filled with light, within which the nearer distance is made measurable by the diminishing scale of the figures, the proselyte pulling off his shirt being about half the height of Christ and the Baptist, the orientals walking beyond him half his size again. On the other side, behind the tree, the ground is pegged with two identical pairs of tree-stumps, and there was, when the landscape was first painted, a third pair in the very foreground, where the Angels now stand. The position of these pegs in the little peninsula made by the river and the diminishing distance within each pair almost enable our eye to measure the tract of meadowland in which they are set.

This sense of proportioned intervals is in tune with the stillness. No ripple in the clear waters of Jordan disturbs the bright reflections. In these the blue sky comes down to earth, proving again the magical clarity of the light which makes the figures radiant. They are planted in it on their firmly foreshortened feet strong as so many columns. The tree is even more of a column, having no comparable base. Piero has no interest as yet in its invisible roots, only in the cylinder of its trunk standing in the circle of the landscape. It gives a scale to the figures and by its plainness emphasises their humanity. In the strength and simplicity of their outlines these are almost sculptures. They are given a remote, hieratic character by the frankness of their poses, the calm of their gestures; even St John's action is suspended. But these very qualities betray the deeply felt tension as they listen to the voice from heaven. Golden rays used to descend from the sky with the Dove. They are largely worn away; but they can hardly have been more than a concession to tradition or popular taste. God is all-pervasive in the quality of the light, inseparable from the cool chord of colour. Just such shades of blue and rose and saffron yellow are to be found in the pictures of Sano di Pietro, a Sienese contemporary of Piero who might well be called the most conventional painter of the century. But, while the colours of Sano di Pietro are almost entirely compositional and decorative, those of Piero are the light itself. Colour and light are here inseparable. In unison they create the atmosphere of the picture, physical and spiritual; and it is no more possible to distinguish the physical from the spiritual than it is the colour from the light.

Longhi, relying mostly it would seem, on some parallel with pictures by Masolino, has consistently held that this is one of the very earliest of Piero's extant works, painted even perhaps before the *Misericordia* polyptych.* This is to say

* Longhi, *op. cit.*, pp. 17–19 and 97.

virtually that Piero sprang from the Umbrian soil with his philosophy almost formed. To look from this picture to *The Nativity* in the same room at the National Gallery is to find there an even greater richness of impression; but in its all-embracing harmony, the essentials of his art are all to be found in *The Baptism*. Already he has brought man, the subtlest and most vital thing in nature, into unison with all her inanimate beauty, her space, her light, her very air; and he has put this system of control into which he had so lovingly persuaded nature to the description of a sacrament in serenely spiritual terms. A philosophy so deep and so wide can have been achieved in the six or seven years after beginning the *Misericordia* picture only by a harmony that was achieved within himself, a balance of observation and of creative thought which cannot be attained in a moment. It must have needed an equally spontaneous enjoyment of all that he daily saw and of all the essential processes of selection and arrangement to reduce the infinite detail of nature to an order of which we are scarcely aware; at least until we begin to ask ourselves how such serenity can ever have been achieved.

7 · Another Visit to Florence?

Thus early in his career as a painter Piero della Francesca had formulated the philosophy which underlies his mature work, and was ready in principle to execute the one great composite monument on the heroic scale which fortune has allowed him to bequeath to us: the decoration of the Principal Chapel in S. Francesco at Arezzo with *Scenes from the Legend of the Holy Cross* and other subjects. Yet it might be misleading to proceed straight to the discussion of the Arezzo cycle. Its scale and completeness represent, for all we know, a new adventure. Given Piero's genius, it is not difficult to understand an achievement like his *Baptism* following upon those of Fra Angelico and Domenico Veneziano. But the larger scenes at Arezzo belong to a scale on which we have no evidence that either of those two had any great success, and which may have been virtually new to Piero himself. They involved infinitely more complicated problems of construction than he is known as yet to have attempted, not to mention the quite unfamiliar themes. As we shall see, he began upon the cycle at Arezzo probably not later than 1454, and that was only ten years from his probable beginning with the *Misericordia* triptych. Perhaps the frescoes at Arezzo in their perfection are the strongest argument for believing that he had already painted at Ferrara on a considerable scale; but the only certain example of his previous practice on the full scale of life is the *Sigismondo Malatesta kneeling to St Sigismund* of 1451; and here it has had to be allowed that he may well have had the active assistance of an architect who took a special interest in just such pictorial problems, while the disposition of no more than two figures was involved.

xv – xxv
28 - 44

24

There is no evidence that, after his casually recorded presence in Florence in 1439, Piero was ever there again, no suggestion that he ever painted there. Yet it would still be virtually a distortion of history not to postulate another visit or visits to the capital of Italian painting before he began to work at Arezzo. Once the idea of such a commission was mooted, he must have been very self-satisfied if he did not wish to see how Agnolo Gaddi a century before had narrated the story of the Holy Cross in the parent Franciscan church of Sta Croce there and how large-scale problems parallel with those which now faced him over its modernisation had been solved by the Florentines who had found themselves the heirs of Masaccio and the subjects of Alberti's exhortations.

Of these the oldest was Paolo Uccello. Indeed, he was probably by a few years the elder of Masaccio, and there is nothing to prove that Masaccio's famous works in Florence were not preceded by something of Uccello's. If Uccello's *Creation of Adam* was indeed painted before any of Masaccio's frescoes, then it was Uccello who in painting first created Renaissance man. His Adam, as he feels the life-blood flowing from the divine touch upon his pulse, and begins to raise his powerfully sculptured body – in that case the first great nude in modern painting – from the bed of flowers among the rocks, gazes back at the Creator with a look of inquiry

10
a and b

which more than hints at the new epoch of humanism. In spiritual and in physical strength Uccello's Adam is the precursor of Michelangelo's. More heroic no doubt was to be Michelangelo's revolt against man's destiny of frustration; but equally individual and infinitely subtle was Uccello's scepticism. In that age of conformity the dynamic quiz which almost every one of his paintings presents to us in a new and startling form must have been disturbing. Probably both these Florentines, so different from each other (especially in that one had too much sense of humour and the other too little), are no less characteristic of the Renaissance than either Masaccio or Piero della Francesca. Neither Uccello nor Michelangelo had any of their serene acceptance of the inborn harmony that made it only necessary for these two to co-ordinate the divine and natural beauty that they felt and saw; and this may be why Uccello, who was scarcely less forward than Masaccio in the power of his outlines, seems to have needed a longer life to develop a comfortable balance in his design.

The Creation of Adam is now the only more or less entire scene of four which he painted in fresco in the *Chiostro Verde*, the 'Green Cloister' of Sta Maria Novella, probably at the outset of his career. The rest are no longer complete as designs and even from *The Creation of Adam* much of the surface has gone, if not all. The green monochrome (*terra verde*), with red skies, may well be only an underpainting in true fresco from which the finishing coat in another medium has scaled away. Not only the outlines of Uccello's early figures but many of his motifs reveal what is confirmed by the records: that, like so many Florentine artists of his generation, he was the pupil of Ghiberti. There is little of the Renaissance as yet in these pictures unless it is the strangeness of their humour and the dynamic power of the fluent drawing and design. Vasari, who marred Uccello's reputation unjustly but permanently, it would seem, by describing him as wholly obsessed with the problems of perspective, calls him on the other hand, 'the first among the old painters to gain a reputation by depicting landscape', and particularly admires his trees. These are indeed the first real trees of modern times, designed with both a new degree of naturalism and a peculiar grace of style which were to be imitated by Domenico Veneziano and developed by Piero himself. Here already they are very much in the third dimension, and at least the halo of the Eternal Father is seen from below as a golden disc in perspective.

As it happens, Alberti's Italian version of the *Della Pittura* coincides in date with Uccello's great monument in fresco to *Sir John Hawkwood* in Florence Cathedral, with its *trompe l'œil* sculptural effect. The picture was an economical substitute for an equestrian statue in the round, and the painter was much less successful in tricking us into the belief that the condottiere and his magnificent charger are carved in marble than he was with the sarcophagus beneath its hooves, raised on three consoles far above our heads. This, however, is very likely not Uccello's fault. It is known that his first effort was not found acceptable and that he had to do the painting again. Perhaps the first time there was too much of the soles of the condottiere's boots and of his horse's belly and not enough of their heroic parts. Perspective could be a very awkward master, and the fact is that Uccello, who was plainly a brilliant geometrician, spent his life in achieving the mastery over it. He can never, unlike some inferior Renaissance artists, have given top priority to its function in creating illusions. Of them all he was the one who believed most in art for art's sake; or he would not have been prepared to paint his foregrounds a bright pink or his horses pale green. The fact that, eventually at least, he painted Sir John Hawkwood's charger as if it were seen more or less at eye level while the sarcophagus supporting it is correctly drawn to be seen from far below, need not prevent us from admiring it to the full. Not only does Uccello's treatment of it demonstrate the adaptability of the art of painting in comparison with that of sculpture; but the animal itself is something new in painting, on the grand scale: the stallion sire of a stud of less splendid but still spirited offspring which were to go into battle on the walls of the Medici Palace in Florence and of S. Francesco at Arezzo.

In spite of these achievements, perhaps Uccello at the time of Piero's recorded presence in Florence in 1439 had not produced much to distract attention from Masaccio's great frescoes in the Carmine Church and in Sta Maria Novella. If Piero returned, however, even in the late 1440s, he must have seen the two later frescoes in the *Chiostro Verde* of Sta Maria Novella comprising four scenes: *The Flood and the Grounding of the Ark, Noah's Sacrifice and Noah's Drunkenness.* Here there is no question of Uccello's mastery of artificial perspective. It is not part of the design, or even its co-ordinating element, merely. It *is* the design. Perspective not only provides the field of the picture and dictates the proportions of everything in the field; it is the instrument of expression. There is no division between the first two episodes. They are presented as one scene, with the ark looming large as some great prison-house on either side. But the wall of the ark on the left, driving back perhaps to the very horizon (the scene has become obscure through damage), draws the eye of the terrified spectator with it, deep into the heart of the hurricane. While the ark on the right, presenting a shorter wall and slewed a little towards the centre as it comes to ground amid the subsiding waters, releases his eye and allows it to rest at the shorter distance. Such is the compelling power of perspective; and the elemental forces which Uccello has created merely with straight lines are amplified by dramatic details like the branches and bunches of leaves which have been blown from their trees and pinned against the ark by the wind.

12a and b

And mankind? Unprepared and inconsequent as ever. One husband at least has taken his wife behind him on a buffalo; 'but, as its hindquarters are sinking', writes Vasari, 'they have not a hope of survival'. And for the most part the men fight each other or exhibit each his pathetic loneliness, trying to keep afloat on a gyrating cask or on too small a raft, or in an inadequate barrel. And the shallows are reached too late for bodies already ballooned with water or eyeless from the depredations of a crow.

Nothing could have been more alien to the spirit of Piero della Francesca than the violence of these scenes or the romantic, playfully cynical invention of their many episodes. Yet here was an electrifying example of the power of perspective carried to extremity. And here, besides perspective as the scaffold for illusions, Piero must, for the first time probably, have encountered an unblushing preoccupation with the geometry of individual items. That object round the neck of the naked youth in Uccello's *Flood*, who seems to be clubbing the drowning horseman in the left corner, would be quite ineffective if it were intended for a life-belt. It is, we are told, the remains of his hat: a *mazzocchio*, the rigid internal structure which maintained the shape of those great turban-caps worn by men of fashion at this period.

Uccello's delight in reconstructing this particular object by a complicated system of projection is evidenced by pen-drawings now in the Uffizi Print Room and recorded by Vasari, who states that he exhibited even more elaborate drawings of *mazzocchi* and was reproached by Donatello for 'neglecting the substance for the shadow'.

Vasari, whose particularly sympathetic life of Piero begins with praise of his drawing of rectilinear bodies and his knowledge of arithmetic and geometry, might have conceded that it was almost certainly Uccello whose experiments of this kind started Piero on the path of study ending in his book on perspective for painters, the *De Prospectiva Pingendi*, and his studies of the regular solids which were plagiarised after his death by his mathematical pupil Luca Pacioli. Uccello himself must have been more or less the pupil of the mathematician Antonio Manetti, with whom, according to Vasari, he was continually discussing the problems of Euclid. The two painters thus form a connecting link between the two mathematicians.

There is a *mazzocchio* too in one of the three scenes of *The Battle of San Romano* which Uccello painted considerably later; but these are pictures which show quite clearly how little he allowed perspective to get the better of him. Painted in oil as decorations for Michelozzo's new Medici Palace in Florence, the three panels are now divided between the National Gallery, London, the Uffizi and the Louvre. They were designed together, probably in the order just given; but we cannot now judge as a whole either the suite of pictures or any single one of them. Originally they had arched tops; but they have been both cut down and extended to make short, wide rectangles, so that the banners and lances are no longer raised up into the sky. It is clear however that, while Uccello used a perspective arrangement of weapons and armour, and even of two horses prone on the ground, to give depth to the field in which the mounted knights above wheel against each other, he allowed them to do this against a grove of roses and orange-trees which serves for a decorative screen as well as a sardonic contrast to the clash of the steel-clad figures. There is high comedy in the furious energy of these robots, in which Uccello has seized the opportunity to combine in happiest unison his interests in human and mechanical forms. Decorations for a palace must be rich and sensuous as well as gay, and for the robots among the roses Uccello, thumbing his nose at Alberti, has laid on the textures of a Gentile da Fabriano, silver and gold leaf pounced with patterns and overlaid with 'dragon's blood' and other translucent pigments. It is no wonder that these records of heroes in battle were catalogued soon after the painter's death as jousting scenes; but their humour and their decorative value and their exquisite craftsmanship should do anything but detract from their seriousness as works of art. Their harmony comes from a complex of design elements synthesised with a skill which leaves no inch of surface without a dynamism of its own and at the same time gives it a clearly defined part in the function of the whole. There is no record to show when these pictures were painted, but a variety of evidence suggests that this was in the second half of the fifties. As we shall see, this means that they are probably rather earlier than the battle scenes by Piero in S. Francesco at Arezzo. We shall find resemblances in conception and design, but these will also show up all the more clearly the contrast between the characters and methods of the two men, especially as it is displayed in the quality of their light. Owing to the deterioration of Uccello's

frescoes and to the mutilation of *The Battle of San Romano* scenes we hardly know
how much significance he attached to light until towards the end of his career
when he produced three enchanting pictures on a small scale which are all excep-
tionally well preserved: *The Hunt by Night* now at Oxford University, *St George and
the Dragon* now in the National Gallery, London, and the *predella* with *The Story of
the Profanation of the Host* at Urbino. In all of these the light is a conscious subtlety, 14a, b
but chronology makes it at least possible that they owe this to the example of Piero. c and
The three little pictures by Uccello are all virtually signed with a crescent moon, d
and the light in them is a brillig of Uccello's own invention, in harmony with the
fantasy of his colour and the whimsical twist which he gives to all his stories. This
is very different from the carefully studied light of day which goes far to create the
serene and serious naturalness of Piero's conceptions.

Nearer to Piero in spirit, not unnaturally, was a Florentine artist of his own
generation, Andrea del Castagno. His series of frescoes painted in the refectory of
Sta Apollonia in Florence belongs probably to a moment soon after Uccello's *Story
of Noah*, and in the great scene with *The Last Supper* which dominates it, Andrea 15
precedes Piero in his acceptance of Alberti's basic ideas, both pictorial and architectural. Indeed his very conception of the scene almost suggests a momentary
obsession with the architectural. His is the prototype of Leonardo's famous *Last
Supper* in Sta Maria delle Grazie, Milan, in its presentation of three walls of an
oblong room seen exactly from the centre; but, whereas Leonardo pays much more
attention to the laws of harmony than to those of nature in the space and the lighting of his scene, Andrea is punctilious in his architectural construction and the
naturalism of his effect. He has represented the room as a loggia under a pantiled
roof, open in front and visible, inside and out, as a whole, even to the wall against
which it appears to be built, and has delineated every detail of its construction and
ornamentation with relentless clarity. We are confronted with one of the long walls
of the room and the table is set parallel with it, so that Christ and the Apostles may
be seated against the three walls. This is the arrangement to be expected, but not
that which Leonardo used; his table is set improbably across a room presented
longitudinally, with regard more to the needs of the design than to the plausibility
of the *mise-en-scène*. Andrea's lighting is also more naturalistic in that a series of
openings in the right-hand wall explains the sideways fall of the light from a single
source upon every one of the thirteen figures. But this is a degree of naturalism
which can be attained by logic rather than by sympathy with nature. The light
is almost like that of a searchlight directed against the opposite wall of the
room, striking upon everything with equal harshness and casting shadows of
undiscriminating black.

The whole of this wall is painted, and over *The Last Supper* is a rolling landscape,
running the entire width of it but continuous only in the sky, where Angels
hover. Two windows separate the three scenes below: *Crucifixion, Entombment* and
Resurrection. The landscape is primitive with stylised trees reminiscent of Byzan-
tinesque mosaics; yet the scene as a whole is made natural by the diffused light, in
contrast with its concentration in the simulated room below. These scenes are
sadly damaged; but in the best preserved, *The Resurrection*, one must recognise
an unmistakable prototype of Piero's *Resurrection* in the Municipio at Borgo
Sansepolcro. Piero will make his picture infinitely more subtle in every respect;

but one must recognise his debt to the fiercely dramatic look of these brilliant eyes in the vividness of the outdoor lighting.

It is in this frescoed wall of Sta Apollonia that Andrea may be said to have found himself. His first dated painting, of 1442, is the remains of some frescoes in Venice, where Uccello had preceded him. Andrea was barely twenty then in all probability, and the frescoes in Sta Apollonia were almost certainly painted while he was still in his early twenties. In *The Last Supper* the classicism of the architecture suggests the influence of one of Alberti's own buildings, and the room is panelled with great squares of marble. But there is no relief from the encrusted ornament, none of the music of Alberti's intervals, none of the gracious balance which Piero was to establish between plain and ornamented surfaces, between solid bodies and the light-filled space which makes their solidity enjoyable. Yet Andrea was before Piero in making a background for his figures out of great panels of green serpentine or purple-red porphyry set in white marble. He used them himself with much more restraint in the elaborate decoration of an actual room at the villa of the Carducci family at Soffiano with a series of life-size Heroes and Heroines, of which most of the remains have been brought to the Castagno Museum in Sta Apollonia. Soffiano is not far from Florence and, if the two painters became acquainted, Piero must have been taken there to admire the grandiose, largely secular scheme which was one of the landmarks of the new development in painting. Piero's only surviving secular picture, the fragmentary *Hercules* now in the Gardner Museum at Boston, Mass., came from the walls of a room in a villa which belonged to him at Sansepolcro. It may well be the remains of a similar scheme on a much more modest scale, and it is possible that Piero had Andrea's Heroes at Soffiano in mind when he carried it out.

In 1456, twenty years after Uccello painted his *Monument to Sir John Hawkwood* in the Cathedral at Florence, Andrea painted a similar memorial on the same scale and on the same wall, to Niccoló da Tolentino. It is more elaborate in conception than Uccello's picture, less decorative in the true sense in spite of an excess of decoration. In the restless flutter of its outlines Andrea could even be accused of initiating the temporary decline of Florentine painting as it is represented by Filippino Lippi. But there is a true dynamism not only in the outlines but in the modelling with light and shade. Andrea's sudden death from plague in the following year is one of the many tragedies of the history of painting. All that he contributed to it was to be consolidated and infinitely refined by Piero della Francesca, but it was to a considerable extent upon Andrea's foundation that Piero worked. It was several years before Andrea's death that he had begun upon the frescoes at Arezzo, but he may well have drawn some of the courage which was needed for the task from Andrea's rough and tragic power. Above all, since Masaccio's untimely death, Andrea alone had painted with the simplicity and grandeur of scale which were now to be Piero's first characteristic.

8 · The Legend of the Holy Cross at Arezzo

XV –
XXV
28 - 44

If the fates have been kindly in preserving for us the frescoes in S. Francesco at Arezzo, it is only by one of their more arbitrary acts that Piero della Francesca ever came to be their painter. The church, at a corner of the minor but convenient square named after the same saint, is typical of the great spare buildings run up throughout Italy during the later thirteenth century and the early fourteenth for the Friars to preach in. It has never been graced with a façade. Fortunately, in the fifteenth century, when the Bacci family, the richest in Arezzo, decided to spend money on the church, they and the Friars thought less of finishing it than of decorating the Principal Chapel. In 1447, apparently after twenty years' delay, the commission was given to Bicci di Lorenzo, an ordinary Florentine practitioner who had been assistant to Domenico Veneziano when he was painting in S. Egidio. The chapel itself is characteristic of Franciscan buildings, roomy, with high, pointed vaulting and with a tall Gothic window facing the arch and the back of the high altar. Since scaffolding was of course necessary, the vaulting had to be painted first. In 1452, when he had all but completed its decoration, together with that of the arch of the window-reveal, and had almost finished painting the entrance arch, Bicci died. There the work must have come to an end for the time being. There is no record of Piero della Francesca's now world-famous frescoes until 1466, when the Confraternity of the Annunciation at Arezzo were commissioning of him a new banner. The contract for this describes Piero as the painter of the main chapel of S. Francesco. Thus there are some fourteen years within which we know that he accomplished – or at least nearly accomplished – what he must have expected to complete in less than eight, according to a contract for an altarpiece which he signed in 1454. It is reasonable to assume, however, that he was prepared to begin without too much delay. In 1454, when he was at Sansepolcro, he undertook the commission for an altarpiece in S. Agostino there, and the eight years which he was given to paint it suggest that he was already bespoken for Arezzo, if not for other work as well. Since this altarpiece was not completed for some fifteen years, there is a probability that he took much longer over the frescoes than he had expected. There was probably an interruption. In April 1459 he was indeed in Rome, painting frescoes in the Vatican Palace. Obedience to a summons from the Pope is anything but evidence, as we know from the story of Masaccio and Masolino, that the work at Arezzo had been completed; but the summons itself perhaps suggests that Piero had by then produced something notable there, that the scaffolding may have been removed from at least one wall. Thus we can be almost certain that his *Scenes from the Legend of the Holy Cross* were taking form during the second half of the fifties. We do not know that they were finished much before 1466, and indeed there is no proof that he was active anywhere else in the early 'sixties.

The scheme for the decoration of the walls is virtually the same as that of Masolino and Masaccio in Florence, with the tiers of scenes on the long walls separated by horizontal bands austerely painted in grisaille to simulate moulded string-courses. Originally, the architecture of the two chapels must have been essentially the same, but the Principal Chapel at Arezzo has escaped the drastic later alterations which truncated and classicised the Brancacci Chapel; and here above the two tiers of rectangular scenes on each wall there is another in the shape of a pointed lunette, its two sides following the curve of the vaulting to meet at the top. At Arezzo too the original decoration has survived in the space between the lowest tier of pictures and the floor: a painted simulation of marble panels in bold colours framed in stone.

These decorative panels are painted freely but with considerable invention, presumably by assistants, in true fresco. They are perfectly preserved, and it is interesting to compare them technically with the scenes above, which are mostly much damaged. Leonetto Tintori, who carried out the most recent cleaning, no doubt with more scientific knowledge and skill than had been used in at least two cleanings and restorations done before, states that the pictures themselves are done in a medium which includes both water and a protein, probably egg. The process of application can best be described as fresco-painting because the final surface of the plaster was applied piece by piece, in order to be painted on while it was still damp, so that a degree of carbonisation of the lime in the plaster resulted. This allowed the colours to be identified with the plaster surface, though it was not enough to fix them completely. The addition of the tempera medium, which limited the carbonisation, must also have slowed up the drying of the plaster, and with it the resulting inconvenient changes of tone. One can see the limitations of the pure fresco method in the brusque painting of Castagno. Piero must have found that it allowed him too little time and involved too much risk of failure in getting the precision and subtlety of tone that he wanted. The outlines of figures and landscapes are pricked, in the traditional way, into the wet plaster through sheets of paper on which they have previously been drawn (cartoons); but the lines of the buildings are in most cases incised directly on to the wall.

To make any just comparison of the impressions made in these two chapels by the pictures themselves will be possible only when cleaning has relieved those by Masaccio of the discoloured surface coatings which now obscure them; but it is probably much more justifiable to attempt it than it would have been if the conditions were reversed. A brown film cannot smother Masaccio's cordial humanity, and it may well have considerably less effect upon the warmer colouring of his draperies and the deeper contrasts of his light and shade. To have known the Arezzo frescoes before and after the recent cleaning is to have had a demonstration of how little it takes in the way of surface accretions to blunt the edges of Piero's more finely cut persons, to fog the clear light in which they shine, to dull all those subtle definitions of colour which make up the brilliant effect.

To walk behind the altar into this chapel and look up at either long wall is to enter into a plateau atmosphere of silvery coolness. On these two walls a notable proportion of the space in each picture is taken up by light blue sky, and on the right wall, that which Piero most probably painted first, there is a tranquil stream winding its way across every scene to catch the blue in its reflections. In the lowest of these scenes, where a river separates the victorious Constantine from the fleeing Maxentius, the blue of the sky is thus brought into the foreground almost to the very edge, as it was in *The Baptism*. Here and there in every scene from the infinite gradations in sky and water a variety of scarcely paler but more solid blues is brought to earth in costumes and accessories; and after the blues come the greys and the whites echoing the floating bars of cloud. The earth is everywhere grey, and there is much black and white throughout. *The Victory of Constantine* is faced by a more lively battle scene on the opposite wall, *The Victory of Heraclius*, and in both these the black and grey of horses and armour alternate under the blue sky with shades of a rather cool chocolate brown. Chocolate was a favourite among the colours with which Greek temples were brightly painted. In Italy it was a rarity even in fresco-painting, and its use by Piero as a foil to colder or more translucent hues is further testimony perhaps to the Greekness of his vision. The remaining colours are few, coming from a simple palette, and often exactly repeated at balanced intervals; but they are used with delight in the variations of the blue or the brown or the green or the red. The green of the costumes is usually shaded with red or warm purple. Many are the shades of violet and rose, their luminosity increased sometimes by juxtaposition with a dull red.

All the scenes on both the long walls of the chapel, including the two battle-pieces, illustrate the Legend of the Holy Cross as it was related in the second half of the thirteenth century by the Dominican Jacopo de Voragine in his *Legenda Aurea*. The quotations below are from *The Golden Legend*, a free translation from the Latin made by William Caxton and printed and published in 1483. Most of the scenes are taken from a chapter, 'Of the Invention of the Holy Cross'. This begins with an account of the death of Adam and the planting upon his grave of a fruit-tree 'which endured there until the time of Solomon', and in the single arched scene at the top of the right-hand wall (facing the window), where Piero himself may well have begun, he has illustrated the three episodes of this prelude. He has joined them in one, as Masaccio did in *The Tribute Money*, and has skilfully filled the potentially awkward upper space with a spreading leafless tree. In *The Baptism* in London he had painted the two leafy walnut trees straight on to the sky with extraordinary freedom, bringing every leaf into three-dimensional existence yet by the sketchiness of his method keeping it subordinate to a single impression, a solid, almost sombre foil to the brilliance of the light. In *The Death of Adam* this one enormous, leafless tree spreading its branches over Adam and Eve and their descendants is wonderful alike in its abstract, sculptured beauty and as a study of complex tree anatomy such as had never been attempted before. Whole but leafless, it presides symbolically over the first and most terrible demonstration that mortality was the lot of all men.

In the smaller scene on the right, where a group surrounds the dying Adam, two of his grandchildren, scarcely comprehending, are splendid in their austerely sensuous physique. The young man, who has his back to us, leans on his heavy staff in an attitude which expresses abstraction by setting at divergent angles the powerful masses of his naked body. The girl, who faces him, stands tensely erect, and the straight lines of the black goat skin hung from her powerful shoulders leave her contours bare and emphasise their magnificent feminity. The strength and beauty and detachment of these two act as a foil to the ultimate ignominy of the flesh, a reminder of all the pride that has gone from the first generation. Eve

4

supports herself with one hand on her stick and with the other helps Adam to raise his head that he may give his last instructions to his already white-haired son. They are completely unselfconscious, the stark realism providing all the pathos.

Seth is to go 'to the gate of Paradise for to get the oil of mercy for to anoint withal his father's body'; and this second episode is touched in with inspiration in the bright light of the distance between the two main scenes. There in the background appeared to Seth 'St Michael the angel, and said to him: Travail not thou in vain for this oil' . . . but 'gave to him of the tree that Adam ate of, and said to him that when that bare fruit he should be guerished and all whole. When Seth came again he found his father dead and planted this tree upon his grave.'

The larger group, surrounding the dead body of Adam in the third episode, is sadly damaged. One sees the little tree, which, in the pathetic hope that it will 'guerish' him, is held to Adam's lips; but, besides one tall, robed figure with his back to us, only the two young people on the extreme left have survived in their entirety. They stand, it would seem, for the continuity of the generations. As they look at each other in awe at the shortness of its term, life becomes particularly theirs.

With the figure of *Hercules* in the Gardner Museum at Boston, painted later on the same scale, these few nudes at Arezzo, set so high on the wall that they would have been difficult to see even if they were much less damaged, are – with the half-nude boy in the tier below – all that we have by Piero in life-size. They are as much as there is by any other Italian painter of this early date; yet the nude was never painted more convincingly or with greater power. In such details as the leg of Adam in the right-hand scene Piero shows his ability to foreshorten when he finds it necessary; but movement is scarcely a part of his art. He may use violent gestures, like that of the woman who flings her arms wide above Adam's dead body, but this is a more or less symbolic pose, to express the cry which cannot be heard. With the great part of his figures their mere presence is enough; so fundamental are the values which they represent. His groups are as natural as the figures which compose them, and have the same close-knit strength.

Over Adam's grave the tree 'endured until the time of Solomon', and Solomon 'because he saw that it was fair . . . did do hew it down and set it in his house named Saltus. And when the Queen of Sheba came to visit Solomon, she worshipped the tree, because she said the Saviour of all the world should be hanged thereon, by whom the realm of the Jews should be defaced and cease. Solomon for this cause made it to be taken up and dolven deep in the ground'.

In the scene below *The Death of Adam*, the first of the four great scenes running the full length of the chapel, two on either side, Piero illustrates two episodes of this story. This time they are more thoroughly separated, as was demanded perhaps by the great width and the rectangular character of the picture-space. This is divided exactly in half at the edge of the plinth to the great loggia of Solomon's palace, and the columns which rest on it shut off the outdoor from the indoor scene. Again, as at Rimini, we see Piero in both scenes describing worldly majesty, and this time, especially in the rather wider open-air scene to the left, there is full play for the processional rhythm with which he liked to express it. Landscape, as always when it is there, sets the scale and the mood of this composition. There is a noble power in the undulations of the mountains behind the royal cortège, which has come to a halt so that the Queen in her cloth of gold under a royal-blue cloak

may kneel to the great balk of hewn timber lying across her path. No more than
half a dozen ladies-in-waiting stand on either side of her train carried by the little
black(?) page who brings up the rear; but they seem a host, representing, for all the
contemporary Italian cut and colour of their gowns, a kingdom of wider spaces
where pulses beat more slowly and there is a statelier measure to the pace of life.
With the clean, long sweep which characterises both their features and their
costume, they make the overdressed and crowded trains of Gentile da Fabriano
and Domenico and Filippo Lippi look fussy and ephemeral. Yet the royal grandeur of these women has its own powerfully conceived foil in the stocky group
behind them, where the two grooms are chatting together as they hold the sturdy
cobs. There are no flowing lines here; man and beast are cut squat and round. But
the cropped manes of the horses introduce the majestic folds in the hills behind,
and the plebeian group is sculptured even more firmly than the other in the light
of a setting sun.

In the adjoining scene of *The Reception by King Solomon* the manners and bearing
of the now white-robed Queen and her ladies so outshine those of Solomon's more
prosaic courtiers that they can only stand and stare. While Solomon wears the gold
brocade mantle of royalty, his court are dressed like the patricians of Arezzo whom
Piero has perhaps portrayed. If one has to turn his back to us, we are compensated
by the noble sculpture of his costume. With his heavy mantle and the great
cappuccio, the hat which requires the *mazzocchio* to keep it in shape, he provides a
vertical landscape of drapery in two shades of rose, while the others reveal each his
own striking individuality. Only Piero's women are always, or very nearly always,
remote. With men he often shows himself a great objective portraitist. The meeting
takes place in a loggia built of sumptuous material. As we look up into its ceiling
we are made aware of its plan, and can freely enjoy the spacious grandeur of its
proportions. If one discounts the breadth of the column which separates it from
the wider landscape, this scene is exactly square, and the proportional relationship
between the two episodes is a fair one.

Long after King Solomon had had the great piece of wood 'dolven deep in the
ground . . . they of Jerusalem did do make a great pit for a piscina, whereas [t]the
ministers of the temple should wash their beasts that they should sacrifice, and
there found this tree . . . And when the time approached of the passion of our Lord,
this tree arose out of the water, and floated above the water, and of this piece of
timber made the Jews the cross of our Lord.' After the passion was over 'this
blessed cross was put in the earth, and hid by the space of a hundred years and
more, but the mother of the emperor, which was named Helena, found it . . .'
St Helena, the discoverer of the true Cross, was at best the first wife of Constantius
Chlorus. They had a son, Constantine, eventually 'the Great'; but Constantius
Chlorus left Helena in order to marry Theodora, the daughter of the Caesar
Maximian. Maximian had a son, Maxentius. In the eventual struggle for the
Empire, Constantine, who had meanwhile risen through his abilities to an outstanding position, was Maxentius' rival. His defeat of Maxentius has always been
considered a turning-point in the history of Christianity, since Constantine afterwards showed great interest in the Church and its affairs and on his death-bed was
baptised – the first Christian Emperor.

So on the lowest tier of this wall, under the story of King Solomon and the

Queen of Sheba, *The Victory of Constantine over Maxentius* in a single episode occupies the whole space. Indeed with characteristic simplicity of conception Piero has cut the picture abruptly against the returning wall at both ends to show that the scene is only part of a great panorama, the score or so of horsemen only fragments of two hosts. According to the Golden Legend, when Constantine had reached the river he was nervous about the result of the battle in the morning, but in a dream he was shown the Cross and promised that it would bring him victory. 'Then was he all comforted of this vision; and on the morn he put in his banner the cross, and made it to be borne tofore him and his host, and after, smote in the host of his enemies and slew and chased great plenty.' Piero has preferred a simpler story and a greater miracle. The river which winds towards us across the plain is to the right of centre in order to show more of the victors on one side than of the vanquished on the other; and here, while trumpets blow and banners wave, Constantine at the head of his troops merely sits on his white charger, holding out the Cross over its head straight before him. Below him the last of the retreating enemy looks cravenly over his shoulder as the roan horse beneath him heaves itself out of the water on to the further bank. The low position, the straining posture of man and beast and the successive curves which they describe away from the centre of the picture are a cunning contrast with the upright stances of the virtuous behind them, with their tall lances rising high above the low horizon, many of them right out of the picture. In the equestrian figure Piero clearly paraphrased in his more powerful language another vividly drawn by Parri Spinelli in a battle scene done in fresco in the Arezzo Badia – perhaps an earlier 'Defeat of Maxentius'. Its remains are now preserved in the Museum in the Palazzo Bruni there.

So low and wide is Piero's scene that it might easily have got out of control had he not respected the idea of a picture surface and kept all the major figures parallel to and close against it. But these are far from being a frieze, for there is a great depth behind them clearly defined. The recession is obtained not only by the foreshortening of the prancing horse on the left, whose muzzle and forelegs are projected up to the very surface; behind him something near to geometry is called into play by the great white ball rising like a balloon above a helmet of which the plumes curve up and away from it against the sky, all within the huge half-cylinders of the yellow and red standard with the black spread-eagle. On the other side the points of the red and yellow dragon pennant of the enemy curve inward like whiplashes towards the distant horizon. Between the rival armies the river winds its way down from distant hills. Reflecting all that it passes, bearing proudly indifferent swans, it tranquilly records another kind of history, the eternal flow of time.

In the pattern made by these standards and the long lances with their pale colours, white, ivory, yellow, even pink and mauve, against the blue of the sky, as well as in the denser frieze of horses' legs, below white and grey and brown, those who are more familiar with the Uffizi or the Louvre or the London National Gallery are apt to see a reflection of Uccello's *Battle of San Romano*. Such evidence as there is about chronology makes it more probable that Uccello's battle scene was painted first; but the two painters had so much the same idea of form and space and their relationship that they might well have hit upon the same device quite independently. What is certain and even more fascinating is that designs which have so much in common formally should be so very far apart in total effect. Piero's low

13a, b and c

horizon and huge sky are all-significant. To look up between the banner and the
ball, beyond the lances into the firmament, is to be drawn into space and bathed in
light. Uccello's knights gleam richly in armour laid with real silver, shaded with a
dark glaze, conceived in terms of the material at least as much as in those of light.
The armoured knights of Piero are sheer painting; and, for all the freedom with
which they had painted, they seem to be the work of the light itself, so brilliantly
do they reflect the sun which is not long risen over the horizon to the left. Changing
their cool tones with every inflection of the surfaces, the suits of steel provide the
sharpest, coldest accents in the picture. Not that Piero ever allows the large fields
of colour which provide its broad contrasts to become monotonous. Their smooth
tranquillity is relieved and emphasised by the finest detail in sharp, bright colour:
jewelled harness, the chasing of an epaulette, the dramatic gleam of eyes punctuates
all the scenes. It is the wondrous variety of the whole which makes its unity so
valuable. Too much contemporary armour would have made it nothing but reflections and given too little opportunity for colour. So several members of the
imperial entourage are dressed, more or less correctly, as Romans, while the first
of eastern Emperors is hatted like John Palaeologus, the last but one, much as he
was portrayed by Pisanello on a medal struck to commemorate his visit to Italy.
Piero could himself have seen the Emperor when he visited Florence in 1439 in an
unavailing effort to reunite the Churches of East and West.

Piero's almost geometrical control of his forms and the musical rhythm of his
colour contrasts are not the only means by which unity is given to so much variety.
Above all, instinct in every colour and thus giving to every form the particular
quality of its substance, binding the forms together as it reveals them, is the
light. Kenneth Clark has described this as 'the most perfect morning light in all
Renaissance painting'.* One could say in all painting before the later nineteenth
century, when Monet and Seurat and Cézanne studied sunlight and its effect on
colour as only Piero della Francesca had done before.

The narrow wall of the chapel at right-angles, the window wall, is also entirely
painted; but the large glazed opening, which rises almost to the top of the vault,
leaves spaces awkward in shape and surfaces very difficult to see. Piero therefore
has himself executed only the two tall narrow scenes of the lowest tier on either
side of the window. This whole wall is dedicated to prophecies, and in the two
irregular spaces at the top, where there is room for no more than a single figure on
either side, he and his assistants or pupils have painted two young *Prophets*. Both
turn to their left, towards the story of the tree on the right-hand wall, as if telling us
where to begin. With their bright, clear gaze, their figures brilliantly lit against a
background, they are reminiscent of Andrea del Castagno, as is the one fully robed
figure in *The Death of Adam*. All the arched pictures of the top tier seem to be the
least mature, and it is possible that Piero, who had begun, probably, with two little
heads which completed Bicci's decoration to the vaulting, worked in the first place
right round the chapel at this height. If, when he began, it had been still entirely
filled with scaffolding for the painting of the vault, this would plainly have been the
most convenient procedure.

The last of the prophecies depicted is, not unnaturally, the most significant of all:
The Annunciation. This is at the bottom on the left. The three others are directly

* Clark, *Piero della Francesca*, 1951, p. 25.

concerned with the Legend of the Holy Cross, each of them representing a prelude to the wide scene adjoining it on the long wall. Thus, below the right-hand *Prophet* is *The Queen of Sheba's Prophecy*, a scene with three young workmen struggling to carry a heavy timber beam. Inevitably they remind us a little of Christ carrying the Cross; but they are in no way Christ-like and there is no Cross as yet; they are carrying the balk for the construction of Solomon's palace. Thinking only of their burden, they do not see the jaws of hell which yawn before their feet, ready to swallow up the whole realm of the Jews, as the Queen of Sheba foretold.* Piero must have made this powerful design; but the execution, which appears to be in pure fresco, can be by no means entirely his, as is easily seen by comparison with the picture below.

This is *The Dream of Constantine*, prelude to the scene of the Christian hero's victory over Maxentius and a fitting complement to it in the conciseness of its vertical design and the closed-in drama of its night effect. As Constantine 'slept in his bed, an angel awoke him, and showed to him the sign of the cross in heaven, and said to him: Behold on high in heaven. Then saw he the cross made of right clear light, and was written thereupon with letters of gold: In this sign thou shalt overcome the battle.' Even in this scene the sky is dominant; for its blackness, engulfing the peaks of the other tents behind, is somehow luminous, and we are aware throughout the scene that night is nature and is receding only in favour of the supernatural. The single tent-pole, round in the hollow of the great red and yellow cone which it supports is, characteristically, off-centre; so that on the left one sees over the top the point of only one other tent beyond, while three can be discerned on the right. But the body of Constantine's tent fills the whole width through most of the tall narrow scene, its roundness providing just the kind of controlled space which Piero often liked to suggest and making this the most sculptural of all his designs. The Angel with his pointing finger comes down like an arrow into the larger circle of his own light between the tent pole and the sleeping Constantine's two sentinel companions, the bearded knight who is to stand beside him in the scene of his victory and the young man who will bestride the plunging horse. The light falls full upon the future Emperor sleeping between his white sheets, and the secretary wakeful at the foot of his bed dressed in a long white coat lined with blue. No cross, no word is necessary. The sudden light is enough.

The story is continued on the same end wall, the other side of the window, in the central tier, above. Converted by the power of the sign which had won him the Roman empire, Constantine sent his mother to find the Cross itself. In Jerusalem Princess Helena met only blank looks and ignorance, until the wise men, threatened with burning, directed her to a youth named Judas. He had inherited from his father a belief in the divinity of Christ and the secret of where the Cross was buried, and he therefore understood the mission of the future saint. But he put patriotism first and warned the wise men: 'beware you all that none of you tell her, for I wot well, then shall our law be destroyed.' He proved more resolute than they, even when Helena said to him: 'By him that was crucified, I shall make thee perish for hunger if thou tell not to me the truth. Then made she him to be cast into a dry

---

* A new interpretation of the scene, the 'jaws of hell' usually being ignored in the commentaries on this picture. Hell was often represented in this literal way.

pit and there tormented him by hunger and evil rest. When he had been seven days in that pit, then said he: If I might be drawn out, I should say the truth. Then he was drawn out . . .' This time it would seem that Piero made only a rough sketch. The scene of Judas pulled out of the dry well displays no more than neat geometry and well ordered light. There is an ingenious architecture in the bare bones of the design; but the very outlines are not sufficiently convincing to make this scene significant according to the high standard of the rest.

Significant far beyond the ordinary measure is the adjoining wide scene in the centre of the other long wall, where Piero with a brilliant economy in story-telling has depicted two episodes: *The Discovery of the Three Crosses* and *The Identification of the Holy Cross* by its power to work miracles. When Judas, released from his pit, 'came to the place, anon the earth moved, and a fume of great sweetness was felt, in such wise that Judas smote his hands together with joy, and said: In truth, Jesu Christ, thou art the Saviour of the world.' The Emperor Hadrian had built a temple on the site, which Helena had first to demolish. 'Then Judas made him ready and began to dig, and when he came to twenty paces deep, he found three crosses, and brought them to the queen, and because he knew not which was the cross of our Lord, he laid them in the middle of the city and abode the demonstrance of God; and about the hour of noon there was a corps of a young man brought to be buried. Judas retained the bier, and laid upon it one of the crosses, and after the second, and when he laid on it the third, anon the body that was dead came to life.' Again, Piero uses a building to distinguish two episodes; and this time it is the end of the pediment of the richly marbled temple directly facing us that falls exactly in the centre of the space.

To the left of this building is a landscape not unworthy of the real Jerusalem in the dormant power of the massive green hills which surround it, with the ploughed fields at their feet. Piero's Jerusalem, crowning the tallest mass, is girt with medieval walls, and from among the gables of its packed white houses with pink or black roofs it thrusts into the blue sky the spires of churches and those tall, square towers which were the pride of the older nobility; he can hardly have failed to have the Jerusalem of Angelico's *Deposition* in mind; yet his presentation of the city and its surrounding hills is modern enough, a link between Renaissance classicism and the pre-Cubist classicism of Cézanne. Together, they form perhaps the strongest of all Piero's landscapes. Cunningly, the shapes of two excavated crosses bind into it the scene of the foreground, where Judas, in white gown and purple hat, oversees the digging before the Empress, her waiting-women and her dwarf. He has become a noble figure, worthy to be baptised as Quiriacus, the future Bishop of Jerusalem.

Again, in the right-hand scene Piero has used the single great Cross with consummate skill both to help create the sense of space and to bind together all the figures within it: the Empress and her kneeling court with the three male bystanders on the other side of the two *dramatis personae*. And here again he has surpassed his own previous efforts and those of any other painter in the clear-cut, foursquare, classical completeness of the design. This is part and parcel with its dramatic concentration, the stillness as all eyes are fixed, all action frozen but that of the dead boy, who suddenly has sat up naked on his bier. His muscular back and bony, outflung arms are profoundly expressive as he returns the firm gaze of Judas, illuminated by a belief that has been freed of fear. Throughout all the scenes on this wall the light now comes from the right, showing that Piero, as Masaccio had done, made use of the actual light from the window to reinforce the illusion of his powerful modelling.

The two scenes above and below are from another chapter of the Golden Legend: 'The Exaltation of the Holy Cross'. Helena left the Cross in Jerusalem; but some three hundred years later it was carried off by Chosroes, the King of the Persians, who 'set the tree of the cross on his right side instead of the sun, and a cock on the left side instead of the Holy Ghost, and commanded that he should be called father'. Heraclius, who had made himself Emperor in Constantinople, went on to defeat the Persians, who threatened his new throne. The Golden Legend gives two accounts of his victory over them. In one of these, while the two armies stood by, he fought a man-to-man duel with Chosroes' son, and then went to Chosroes, who 'knew not the end of the battle . . . found him sitting on his siege of gold' and offered to let him keep his throne if he would be baptised. 'And when he would not accord thereto, he did anon do smite of his head, and commanded that he should be buried because he had been a king.' In the other account Heraclius 'destroyed and wasted the Persians with many battles that he made to them, and made Cosdroe to flee into the city of Ctesiphont'. Here he was killed by his own son, who made alliance with Heraclius and finally sent him 'the tree of the cross and all the prisoners'. In both accounts Heraclius restored the Cross to Jerusalem.

The Return of the Cross to Jerusalem is the subject of the single episode which fills the arched space at the top of this wall and must, according to its position, have been painted at least before the scenes of the tiers below. Like the scene facing it, it has been severely damaged. The leading figure bearing the Cross is defaced and the landscape which once filled the centre to the low horizon is entirely lost, except for the tall tree thrusting its cone of greenery into the rich colour of the sky. This is painted in just the same manner as the foremost tree of *The Baptism* in London, much more freely than the others in these frescoes. Quite enough of *The Return of the Cross* remains, however, in proof of Piero's hand, both in the design and in the execution. The problem of the awkward height is solved again by trees; but the two are subordinate to the clean shape of the tall Cross between them, with its foreshortened arms. The noble group of earnest men behind it is made taller by their hats of geometrical design. Those on the receiving side have taken off their headgear as they fall on their knees before the Cross; but this reduction of their group in height is more than compensated in the design by the dramatic perspective of the great red wall of the city with its towers rising at intervals above them to catch the light. Devotion is in the movement of their hands and the set of all their heads, and shines in their highly individual faces. At their back, emerging into the sunlight from the shadow of the wall, the elder in a white mantle who takes off his hat as he begins to kneel is good witness of Piero's power in figure-design and characterisation.

The two episodes which precede all this, *The Victory of Heraclius* and *The Execution of Chosroes*, are shown together in the last wide scene, in the lowest tier. Piero has ignored the possibility offered by Voragine of limiting the fight to a duel in the lists under the eyes of two hosts pledged to non-intervention. He has chosen instead to represent a ferocious free-for-all, which again he extends in our imagination beyond the visible scene by cutting figures off abruptly at either end. Even in the execution episode on the right, the raised sword of the executioner and one of his legs disappear against the return of the window wall. Similarly, the two episodes themselves overlap, the hind legs of a horse kicking into the very centre of the execution scene from the *mêlée* which precedes it. Thus we are plainly intended to look at the whole tier as a single composition. That it is also part of a running frieze, endless and without the pause and interval which Piero has used in all the other wide scenes, has caused him to make this composition the most intricate and the most closely knit. Here only the poles of the few great heraldic banners are upright. The air is criss-crossed with flying shafts and down below, among the close-packed bodies, the roundness of heads and head-dresses is cut across in every direction by the sharp diagonals of raised weapons, of maces, swords and daggers, and lances mostly splintered.

The invention of the design is endless. However arbitrary one's choice in isolating a portion from the vast rectangle of this scene, it will be found to be a fascinating pattern of contrasted shapes and colours. But the pattern is always of living outlines, giving movement and full relief to the shapes, which glow with colour and light; for every detail of the picture, every form that Piero invents, whether it is a horse or a piece of harness, a man or his weapon or his fantastic headgear, whatever it is, it exists in the light which he has created with it, absorbing or reflecting it. In and out of this dense mass of forms, animate and inanimate, the light is always there, reflected by each and all and filling every space between.

As usual just off centre, the nodal point of the design is the oval shield of the foot-soldier, quartered so that the lines which cross in it provide literally the crux: the crux of who knows what complicated geometric scheme in disguise, for disorder could not be so firmly ordered if there were not an armature of geometric calculation. It is also the centre of a little vacuum into which men and horses are pressing from the back and sides. Not all of them, for the climax is elsewhere. It is on the extreme right of the battle that Heraclius, as if performing an act of pre-ordained ritual, stabs the son of Chosroes in the throat. The packed confusion ends above his already closing eyes, at the only clear space, under the canopy of his father's empty throne. The royal blue mantle of Chosroes is the deepest note of colour in the infinite range which makes this picture the most elaborate of the series; and the canopy over his throne offers the sheerest pleasure in the play of the light across its backcloth of rose-coloured damask. It is all-important in the whole design, this empty canopy. Men and horses and weapons are fitted so close in a great frieze that we are allowed no glimpse of landscape, either behind or in front; but the depth of the canopy arch gives definition to the whole space, and the standards over the battle can be seen to be on a line behind it and curving deeper still into the infinity of the sky.

In front of the dais, below the set faces of those who have condemned him, the infidel king kneels in philosophic resignation. No less than with the courtly Velazquez, no man in any picture by Piero is without nobility. Indeed Chosroes is virtually identical with the Eternal Father of the adjoining *Annunciation*. It is part of Piero's classicism that he is ready to use the same archetypes quite often in different contexts. By the same token it would have seemed to him unclassical to depict a pitiable expression on a face. There is a larger, more magnanimous drama in the presentation of this empty throne raised between Cross and cock above the crowd of enemies surrounding the abased king. Among the stony-faced bystanders, according to Vasari, are the donor Luigi Bacci and several brothers.

The Annunciation, at right angles to *The Execution of Chosroes*, at the foot of the window wall, is particularly difficult to see, there being no powerful contrast of light and shade as there is in its counterpart, *The Dream of Constantine*. It could not be pretended that the light in the picture comes from the great window, which pierces the wall on which it is painted; but Piero must have felt that the actual light from this source in the spectator's eye would cause confusion if the painted light came from the opposite direction. Thus, though there is a great rectangle of sky at the top on the left from which the Eternal Father sends down blessings upon Mary's womb, even his face is lit from above on the other side, like the Virgin's palace itself and everything which its walls enclose. In the picture every surface reflects light, the bar across the open window above throwing a slight shadow on to the reflecting wall below, as it might in a domestic scene by a Dutch painter of two centuries later. But Piero's light has the Mediterranean clarity, and it falls upon marble cut sharp and clean in the tradition of the Greeks. One feels that if any part of this graceful building were tapped with a hammer, there would be a clear metallic ring.

The Angel and the Madonna have much the same poses as Piero had given them more than ten years ago in the *Misericordia* polyptych; but they have become greatly sophisticated. With the Madonna it is only a trace of personality which gives character to the elliptical shape of her head, repeated more vaguely below the column of her neck in the flatter curves of her blue mantle, sweeping and grandiose in contrast with the more complex and subtler folds of the rose gown beneath. But, if the remoteness of her facial expression is brought about by the bare concealment of the formal construction, this is far from the case with the strong hands freely expressive of her resolution. It had been the tradition for some two centuries to make the announcing Angel discover the Virgin like this, reading in the loggia of a palace; but to look back at a succession of other Annunciations is to realise more clearly the compactness and precision of this picture in its three-dimensional design. The contrast between the richly ornamented plane at the back of the scene, parallel with the picture surface, and the forward movement of the loggia provides with all simplicity the pleasure that is to be had from space defined and filled with light. The shapely column supporting the corner of the palace, which traces a line down the centre of the picture surface, with its base against that and its twin against the wall behind, fulfils the Alberti commandment of establishing clearly the depth of the picture space. The beams which the two columns support provide the only strong orthogonals, and these lead our eye directly to the Virgin's face. The strength and simplicity of this construction enable Piero to overlay it not only with rich colour but with intricate patterns, like the Gothic tracery of the intarsia on the door behind the Angel and the lively, more up-to-date perspective pattern of double cubes, now rather out of tone with the rest, which seem to decorate the head-board of the Virgin's muslin-curtained bed. Indeed, with these he provides fields of vibration between the plain reflecting surfaces, just as the subtle curves of the column rise up in the very centre of a host of straight lines.

There remain only two fragments of Piero's painting on the pilasters supporting the choir arch: on one side the upper part, much worn, of a once full-length figure of *St Peter Martyr*, on the other the head and shoulders only of a brilliant *Archangel* in white against a background of serpentine.

The unity which Piero has given to the Arezzo frescoes as a whole by his respect for the need of a total decorative effect, by the harmony of his colours and the consistency of his lighting, the simplicity and the grandeur of the scale, make it easy in retrospect to forget the stimulus of their variety. Indeed, the harmony between them makes the more remarkable the fundamental novelty with which he conceives every new scene, the continual freshness of his invention.

Perhaps *The Legend of the Holy Cross* was fixed upon not merely as an old Franciscan favourite which had proved a good subject for painters. Perhaps fable and history were invoked and the living Palaeologus identified with Constantine in order to rouse interest in a unification of the two Christian churches and in a new crusade against the Turkish infidel. The choice of subject was almost certainly made, however, long before Piero took the place of the chosen painter; and this was not his kind of problem. If he ever allowed himself to be personally involved in the story that he was painting, it was in the sentence pronounced upon Adam and his posterity. No doubt it was not only the poor lighting available that made him leave to the execution of assistants the two ignoble subjects, the torture of the pit and the blind self-destruction of the Jews. His problem lay beyond the story; it was that of the philosophers of this great period: to discover the proof of God in the laws of nature, to find the rules of her invisible harmony, and in his paintings to make this visible. But the principal medium through which nature could attain perfection was man; and while we are looking at Piero's men and women, the lords-creator of their own noble spaces, we are almost convinced that this is true.

THE SCENES FROM THE LEGEND OF THE HOLY CROSS
S. Francesco, Arezzo

XVIII

XX

XXI →

XXII →

XXIII

XXV

9 · Rome and Urbino

Aeneas Silvius de' Piccolomini, who was elected Pope Pius II in 1458, was the great humanist Pope. His *Commentaries* form one of the most illuminating of auto-biographies, for he was unique among the pontiffs of the century in his combination of an appealing zest for life with wide learning and an urgent political realism. He proceeded at once to summon the rulers of Europe to a Council concerning the danger from the Turks, to whom Constantinople had fallen in 1453. But before they met at Mantua in 1459 Pius had already got a number of artistic projects under way. The beautiful miniature city of Pienza was to rise out of his birthplace in Southern Tuscany and all good artists of the region were to profit from his patronage. To Piero's contemporaries his summons by Pope Pius II to Rome must have been the great event of his life. Alas, the summons itself is unrecorded, there are only two contemporary records of this visit, one a document, the other a picture, and both are sadly incomplete. The document, dated 12 April 1459,* a Vatican order for 150 florins to be paid to him 'for part of his work on certain paintings he is doing in the room of the Holiness of our Lord', bears out Vasari's statement in his life of Piero that he painted 'two scenes in the upper rooms' in the Vatican Palace. Vasari mentions that Piero finished them; but in his life of Raphael, who painted over them, he states, perhaps in extenuation, that only one composition had been completed. Apparently the site was the room made famous by Raphael as the *Stanza di Eliodoro*.

The extant painting, in the great church of Sta Maria Maggiore, at the other end of Rome, went totally unrecorded; indeed it was recognised as the work of Piero only in recent times. The Chapel of S. Michele, which it partly decorates, has been no more than a side porch, probably since 1605, when the Baptistry which it now serves was built by Paul V. Decorating the vault above the wall now containing the outer door, the *St Luke* has been less subjected to draughts than the other three Evangelists. There are remnants of a *St Mark*(?) on the opposite vault; but of the other two nothing remains but some fragments of the bold Greek ornament, typical of Piero, which once surrounded all four panels. The walls were no doubt painted too; but the only surviving composition, a *Dead Christ supported by Angels*, though worthy of study, is not by Piero's hand. *St Luke* is identified by his winged bull, whose bold shape has survived like the finely idealised head and hands of his master. The Saint's voluminously draped body is much damaged, and although it is more than forty years since Longhi drew attention to this noble figure, drawn with great power, nothing has yet been done to improve its ignominious condition.

Vasari states that it was as he left Rome that Piero lost the mother who had brought him up, without the aid of husband and father, from birth. Romana had come to Sansepolcro as a bride from the little hill town of Monterchi nearby. An early widowhood would make it likely, even if she had brought up Piero and his

27

* Reproduced by G. Zippel in *Rassegna d'Arte*, 1919, pp. 87 ff.

brother at Sansepolcro, that at least she had often returned to Monterchi and that she now chose to be buried there. Such a story would explain the fresco by Piero in the chapel of the little cemetery outside Monterchi. It would also account for the originality of its theme, chosen and perhaps devised by the painter himself. Known
as *La Madonna del Parto*, the 'Virgin of Birth', the picture represents neither death nor resurrection but the continuity of life.

On the walls of the older churches all over Italy are to be found sculptured sepulchral monuments with two Angels drawing aside curtains to reveal the recumbent effigy of the deceased. From this memorial tradition of three centuries Piero has adopted for his *Madonna del Parto* the Angels and the curtains. But in his picture what is revealed, instead of death supine, is the erect and sturdy promise of new life. There is really but one curtain, forming the sides of a pavilion fit for an empress, a splendid cylinder of gold and crimson damask, lined, like the sheltering mantle of the *Madonna della Misericordia*, with grey fur. As the Angels part it, holding the two hems high above their heads, it forms a wide ogive arch to frame the goddess who towers above them, brilliantly fresh and dressed in the fur-lined gown of light blue stuff of a patrician housewife. She is strong and impersonal as nature; but she promises, as nature promises with the bursting pomegranate, that she will make new life. The effect of the unveiling is spectacular. But the shock is relieved by the tranquilly expectant power of this woman and the sheer symmetry of her setting. Of course, the apex of the curtain arch is off centre; the light, coming from the left to show the brilliance of the pale head, makes the gold in the damask glow bright on that side and but dimly on the other; the reversed colours of the Angels, one in a green tunic with scarlet hose and rose-coloured wings, the other in a rose tunic with hose and wings of different greens, are not by any means identical. But the opening is an almost perfect arch; the figure of the damask is twice repeated on either side; the Angels are posed exactly in reverse, their outlines even pricked upon the wall, apparently, from the same cartoon. By what simple devices can a great artist turn a principle of nature into a revelation!

In the *Madonna del Parto* it is only the three haloes which claim for Christianity a theme which has no more a time than a place. Piero's religion is wider than any creed, and it has an earthy, primordial quality, revealed clearly when the theme is the rebirth of the spirit. His return from Rome seems a likely enough moment for
the City of Sansepolcro to have commissioned him to paint *The Resurrection* in their public palace, the *Palazzo dei Conservatori* or *Pretorio*. This is now the Municipal Gallery, and the fresco is still there, though its position has been changed, either in 1480, in Piero's lifetime, or early in the next century. The palace is opposite the cathedral, and to study the traditional design for his theme Piero had only to cross the street. The beautiful high-altarpiece there, from a Sienese studio, shows a rose-clad Christ rising in majesty with one foot on the front of the sepulchre, looking straight before him. Piero had only to translate the theme further into terms of three-dimensional actuality. He has sited the tomb at the foot of hills more wild than those in *The Baptism*; his Christ, now more mature and classical – and more like Castagno's – is again exactly in the centre. The attitude is no longer one of submission; the eyes are now turned straight upon us, penetrating our thin pretences.

No use in this simple, urgent presence to speak anything but truth. Alert with all-seeing intention, the risen Christ wears his shroud like a toga, and the red cross on his militant standard is repeated in large by the composition. The tomb makes a pale horizontal bar right across the scene and the pole of the standard, which he has stood almost vertically on the ground before it, reaches to the very top. The leg which he plants beside it on the edge of the tomb proclaims his vital power, and no detail of form, even in Greek sculpture, has a cleaner strength than this foot and ankle emerging from the cave of drapery. The brilliance of the ivory torso and the rose-pink shroud is emphasised by the deep colours worn by the Roman soldiers, shades of purple and turquoise set off by bronze and a touch of scarlet. One of the soldiers is awakened and staring, the others still blind in sleep. According to Vasari, it was Piero's custom to model figures in clay before he drew them, and it is easy to believe that this was one of the means by which he achieved the perfection of this group. The Roman costume allows him to give the third dimension to his forms with even more precision and clarity than usual. There is air and light round every one; but together they are bound by rhythmical movement into a living pyramid which has its effulgent apex in Christ's head. The trees converging round it in the still darkened landscape are bare on one side and on the other rich in foliage. Piero's symbolism is always elemental.

The authorities of Sansepolcro became so proud of this picture that they had it removed from a side wall and set immediately opposite the entrance. It is composed as if the centre of it were on a level with our eyes; but we know that we were intended to look up to it, as we do now, from the perspective of the white stone frame which Piero painted round it on the wall. Fluted Corinthian columns stand on a deep base bearing a now damaged inscription, and originally no doubt supported architrave, frieze and cornice of an equal elegance. Unfortunately the frieze and cornice have been destroyed, together with a vertical strip from the outer part of each column. In the picture itself sky and landscape are somewhat damaged; but this is on the whole the best preserved of Piero's compositions in fresco.

His presence at Sansepolcro in 1460 was formerly attested by an inscription at the foot of another fresco in the Gallery, *St Louis*. This is in rather ruinous condition now, the edges of the composition being gone from all four sides and the figure no longer existing below the knees. It was cleaned and made more presentable about 1950. The inscription, once at the foot, stating that it was painted in 1460 during the rectorship of the Florentine Lodovico (Louis) Acciaioli, was transcribed by Dragomanni in 1835: TEMPORE NOBILIS ET GENEROSI VIRI LODOVICI ACCIAIOLI PRO MAGNIFICO ET ECCELSO POPVLO FLORENTINO RECTORIS AC PRIMI VEXELLIFERI IVXTITIAE AERE BVRGIANO MCCCCLX*. Longhi removed this picture from its traditional place in the list of Piero's authentic works and most writers have followed him; but Clark has very properly restored it. There could hardly be a better illustration of Piero's ability to establish the authority of his subject by the simple, uncompromising severity of his design, and the Florentine Governor of Sansepolcro could not have wished for a Patron Saint who expressed more convincingly his own intended zeal in the administration of justice.

It may have been at about this time that Piero began to paint easel-pictures for Urbino, on the other side of the mountains from Arezzo, looking towards the

48

* F. Gherardi-Dragomanni, *Vita di Pietro della Francesca del Vasari*, 1835. The reference is given by Longhi and others.

Adriatic. The small state of which the city of Urbino was the capital was to be swallowed up all too soon by the Papacy; but during Piero's lifetime it reached its zenith under Federico di Montefeltro, last but one in direct descent of a long line of lords of a domain which he considerably extended, partly at the expense of Sigismondo Malatesta. For a brief moment he made Urbino one of the powers of the land, and a great centre of Renaissance culture. King Henry VII of England sent him the Garter. Baldassare Castiglione called him 'the light of Italy'.

Federico won his great position as a *condottiere*; but what gave special value to the greatest soldier of his day was his habit of keeping faith. He was consequently never without a prodigious retaining fee, sometimes from the Pope, sometimes from a league of states, usually from the King of Naples. This he spent at home, ruling, in grandeur but with personal austerity and a unique degree of accessibility, over a people whom he hardly had to tax. 'Ever careful', according to his contemporary biographer, Vespasiano, 'to keep intellect and virtue to the front and to learn some new thing every day', he was sometimes described, not without bias perhaps, as the most learned man of his own learned court. His famous library, 'where all the books are superlatively good, and written with the pen, and had there been one printed volume it would have been ashamed in such company', was not second even to the Vatican's, to which most of it was eventually added. We owe to his patronage many of the first translations from the Greek. His great palace at Urbino, built by a despot who had nothing to fear from his people, is probably the first such building to have virtually no fortification. Its rose-red brick and white stone smile on one side upon the country below it and on the other upon the main piazza of the little town. To step from this into the arcaded Court of Honour is to believe that here was the domain of reason and order. To walk from one spacious and lofty room to another or out on to a balcony between the ornamental towers is to be persuaded that the greatest pleasures were those of enlightenment.

The spirit of the palace is so much the spirit of Pietro's pictures that many art-historians have come to believe that he had to do with the building of it. At intervals some writer credits him with two perspective pictures of ideal cities, one still in the Palace at Urbino, the other in Berlin–Dahlem. Each one a harmony of stately buildings, designed as a homogeneous unit, free alike of traffic and advertisement, but also even of humanity, these are indeed Utopian in idea; but they are drab in colour and lacking in pictorial quality, either in their design or in their execution. The authorship of Francesco di Giorgio, who came to Urbino later as architect and engineer, is equally ruled out; the delicate fantasy of his ideas and of his touch in pictures is well known. The author must have been a non-painter: Luciano Laurana perhaps, the architect and sculptor.

Federico had had the work on the palace begun before 1460; but what was at first only a richly ornamented building in the Renaissance style seems to have become an ordered expression of the new classicism only after 1465, with the arrival of Laurana. It was he almost certainly who designed those parts of the palace, including the Court of Honour, which are of the purest beauty. Piero's services as a painter are not known to have been used in the decoration of the palace, and, when it came to the adornment of Federico's own sanctum, it was the Netherlander Justus of Ghent who was commissioned to paint the series of

portraits of illustrious men now divided between Urbino and the Louvre, 'because', 115
according to Vespasiano, Federico 'could not find painters in oil on panel to suit
his taste in Italy'.

18a
and b

That Piero's treatise *On Perspective in Painting* was dedicated to Federico could
mean merely that he wanted a copy preserved in the great library; but, when he
later dedicated his little book on the *Five Regular Bodies* to Duke Guidobaldo, who
had succeeded in 1482, he claimed that he had given his best to the father without
stint. Vasari is almost certainly wrong, however, in suggesting that Urbino was
where the painter first made a reputation.

The only picture by Piero which has remained at Urbino continuously was XXXI-
brought to the Palace from the Cathedral sacristy. It is hard to believe, however, XXXIII
that it was not painted either for Federico or for some member of his court. It is 25
the supreme achievement of perfectionism. Its scale is that of a private chapel or
room. Its theme is evidently one of personal choice. Indeed the subject was all too
soon forgotten, and the question of the picture's date has been bedevilled by
acceptance of an irrelevant local legend, dating only from the eighteenth century.
This identified the three figures of the foreground as Federico's predecessor and
half-brother, Duke Oddantonio, between two of the evil counsellors who led him
towards his untimely end; whereas the youth in the middle, barefoot and dressed
in a simple tunic of deep rose, has the radiant face of Piero's Saints and Angels, and
it is a learned philosopher who is expounding some theme to one of the princes of
the world, dressed in fur-lined robe and mantle of royal blue damask heavy with
gold thread. Clark* has suggested that these persons somehow represent one of the
Christian councils, like that called by Pius II at Mantua in 1459, which were vainly
convened against the Turk. Thus the Flagellation of Christ in the loggia behind
would symbolise the recent tribulations of the Church. Clark himself has described
the youth as Arcadian, and the subject of the conversation may be less topical than
he suggests. But he is plainly right in the broad conclusion that a conversation
is going on between contemporaries about some magnanimous theme to which
Christ's sufferings fourteen centuries ago are somehow relevant. *An Allegory, with
the Flagellation of Christ* is perhaps the most appropriate title for the picture.

On the dais beneath Pilate's throne is the signature OPVS PETRI DEBVRGO
SCI SEPVLCRI (the CR in monogram); but, alas, no date. The identification of
Oddantonio seemed to point to a date even in the 'forties, and Clark, who was the
first to point out the absurdity of the identification, has gone no further in im-
proving the date than to draw a parallel with the earlier frescoes at Arezzo. Many
writers have made a comparison with one of these, *The Discovery of the Holy Cross
by the Queen of Sheba and her Reception by Solomon*, because the loggias in the two
pictures are broadly similar and in each the loggia scene is combined with one in
the open air; but, if comparisons can be relevant between two pictures so different
in scale and in theme, then there must have been an interval between them long
enough to allow a marked development and refinement of Piero's art.

Whereas in the fresco the outer row of columns starts at the picture surface and
is used to separate two distinct stories, in the *Allegory* it is set at a calculated
distance well into the picture space, as the central feature of a single composition.
Indeed it might be called the key to Piero's solution of the puzzle set him by his

* Clark, *op. cit.*, pp. 19–20.

patron, a problem of simultaneous division and unity: how to distinguish two groups in time and space while uniting them in the concentration of a perfect picture. This challenge to his powers of harmonisation resulted in the most sophisticated of all his works. His imagination carried him far beyond the bare necessities of the subject dictated. One of the elements giving a universal significance to this scene, whatever its subject, is the suggestion of infinity, and this called for something more elaborate than the juxtaposition of a covered and an open court. On the other side of Pilate, through one of the loggia's nobly proportioned doors, can be seen a staircase drenched in sunlight. The further wall of the staircase must mark the end of that building, because behind it the light comes flooding from the left into the court. Beyond this open space is another loggia on the second storey, and beyond that again the wall which separates the court from the world outside.

Such architectural perspective as this Piero must have worked out for the picture from a ground plan, and perhaps an elevation, drawing as if he were going to construct actual buildings, achieving the harmony of the various parts by the use of a single unit of measurement. To read the procedure backwards, rediscovering the plan which Piero drew and the all-important key to its unity of proportion, requires expertise in the technique of perspective. The solution has been published by R. Wittkower and B.A.R. Carter*. The plan and elevation which they reproduce do not go beyond the back wall of the loggia, but by comparing them with the picture it can be deduced that everything else is to scale. Carter has shown that, as the tiles which pave the entire picture-space suggest, the ground-plan has been worked out in squares, small and large, and that the squares of the loggia's coffered ceiling correspond exactly with those of the pavement below. He has discovered that the unit, or modulus, is half the length of the sides of the small terracotta tiles and a third of the width of the white marble bands which separate the large squares into which these are grouped; and that the proportional placing of the figures is governed by the same unit. Thus figures and architecture are integrated into one system of spatial relationships. The writers, moreover, have found 'good reason to believe' that the unit adopted is that twice given in the margin of the treatise *De Divina Proportione* by Luca Pacioli, who became notorious for publishing Piero's mathematics as his own.

Though the black and white marble pavement of the loggia is part of the same scheme, it has a character of its own which Wittkower shows to be significant in emphasising the symbolic nature of the Flagellation scene. He considers that the great circle of black marble in which Christ's column is placed is itself a symbol of Christ, and suggests that the cruciform pattern within the squares before and behind it is derived from a polygonal division of the circle, a problem which Piero investigated in his *Five Regular Bodies*.

When all this had been worked out on plan and elevation, it still had to be translated in terms of perspective to the picture surface; and it is only when the resulting design had been scored in the gesso of the panel that the painting began. Nevertheless it is the precision, the order, the harmony of proportion, the unity of these underdrawn calculations which make the world of light and colour painted over them a dream world of reason and enlightenment.

* R. Wittkower and B.A.R. Carter in the *Journal of the Warburg and Courtauld Institutes*, XVI, 1953, 3–4, pp. 292–302.

Piero begins his earlier book *On Perspective in Painting* by dividing the art, as Alberti had done, into three parts, which he calls design, measurement and colour. All his three words are refinements of Alberti's, and it is significant that, when Alberti wrote 'distribution of light', as one might when thinking of Masaccio, Piero has written merely 'colour'. This is no simplification. Piero knew that light can be rendered with subtlety only by the quality of colours, that light and colour in painting are the same thing. And so one can but describe the colour design of this picture broadly in terms of light. In the Queen of Sheba fresco the interior and exterior scenes are held together by light from a single source, sweeping across the landscape into the loggia. In the *Allegory* the light comes from the same side, from the left; but the loggia is reversed; it has its back to the light. Piero had discovered early in his career the superior intensity of colour in reflected light, and here the scene of the Flagellation is enacted in light which comes from the other direction, reflected sideways from the buildings and upward from the pavement of the court. Hence the sheer beauty of the half-light in the coffered ceiling and the exquisite subtleties of colour within the loggia, mostly brighter, but muted in their brilliance so that they are in harmony with the heavier colour of the figures standing in the light outside.

The idealist theme of this picture, the classic, mathematical design, the clarity of the mind that conceived it and of the Mediterranean light which fills it prevent us from thinking at once of Vermeer and de Hoogh, the Dutch domestic painters of the seventeenth century; but everything that they did is already here, and more. The incidence of the light is as carefully reasoned as the architectural framework. The sun, high on the left, falls full upon the foreground, while the middle part of the court is in shadow from the loggia. Further back, however, the pavement of the court is brilliant again with light which informs us of the open space behind the loggia. Beyond the courtyard wall there is scarcely more than a glimpse of blue sky. Yet the luminosity of the whole scene seems to depend upon the translucency of this heavenly element, into which the earth thrusts up the dark mass of the fruit tree, greedily swallowing the light among the myriad shadows and reflections of its solid, glossy leaves. The tree is not there only for this contrast of elements. Its absorbent darkness makes more radiant still the face of the Arcadian listener in the foreground. We are left with the Giorgionesque mystery of these three men and the subject of the conversation. We read its significance in the presence of the Arcadian, in the intensely glowing countenance of the earnest expositor and in the high status of his listener.

While the incised lines of the architecture prove that the elaborate rectilinear design of the *Allegory* was fixed before any painting began, minor changes in the contours of the figures show not only that these were painted last but that the creative process continued to the end. Though in the deeper colour of the draperies the strokes of the brush are fused together, most of the painting can be seen to be done with the finest of brushes in minute hatching strokes which make it almost certain that the medium is egg tempera. In the finishing of the picture pains were no more spared than in its design.

In the other picture by Piero now at Urbino the Dutch character has often been XXIX - XXX 66 remarked. This is *The Madonna and Child with two Angels* which has been brought from Sta Maria delle Grazie at Sinigallia on the Adriatic coast. There is no early record of it there and, since the little seaport became joined to Urbino before long by inheritance, this picture also may well have actually originated in the capital. It has always been placed by writers among Piero's very last works, and there is indeed about it the same sweet air of contentment that sets the mood of *The Nativity*. But *The Nativity* is painted, albeit with a magical deftness, loosely in oil paint. The Sinigallia *Madonna* is painted tightly, with the same hatching strokes just remarked in *The Allegory with the Flagellation*, though more boldly, in accordance with the larger scale. These too suggest the use of pure tempera, which we shall find Piero abandoning in favour of an oil and tempera emulsion by 1469. There is no material reason why a painter should not revert to tempera after he has painted in oils; but there would seem to be no physical or psychological reason why Piero should have used again at the end of his life a technique evolved for a tighter kind of painting, which would be more exacting to ageing eyes and less suitable for achieving the effects of luminosity which are the essence of this picture.

As far as the all-significant rendering of the light is concerned, this is only more obvious here than in the *Allegory* because the effect is much simpler and broader and because the composition reminds us of Netherlandish oil paintings in which this element is studied more consciously than anything else. Piero may well have had some northern prototype in mind, which would make it all the more remarkable if he painted this picture in tempera – as it seems that he did – *after* he had become accustomed to using oils. Of all the Madonnas of the early Italian Renaissance this is the least exotic, the most domestic. The box and the basket of linen on the alcove shelves show the scene to be a corner in an elegant house, and nothing could be more intimate, somehow, than the kiss of the sunlight upon the wall of the little closet behind. The Virgin has no halo, and we are very close to her, with no parapet between us, as there is in all those Madonnas by the Venetian Giovanni Bellini, who had already been painting now for some years. The Virgin is built as strongly as ever, easily supporting on her arm a Child like the infant Hercules; but she is the softest and most personal of Piero's few Madonnas. This is, incidentally, the only work by him – except for small figures on the pilasters of frames – in which the figures are in half-length. The indoor light is rendered by quiet colour: the Virgin's plain gown, in design like that of the *Madonna del Parto*, a deep rose, her mantle an unusually dark blue, the Angels in light blue and light rose. As always, there are bright, sharp touches, like the exquisitely painted coral necklace of the Child; but the remainder, including the lining of the mantle, is in shades of white and grey, though the cold grey of the *pietra serena* is relieved by greenish woodwork and pale gold. This glints in the hair and the ornaments, and the sun lays it in generous patches on the wall of the little room beyond.

The chronology of Piero's pictures at Urbino is confused in other ways. In 1466 the Carmelite Ferabó wrote a Latin poem entitled 'The Likeness of the Prince painted by Piero of Borgo addresses the Prince himself', and it is usually accepted that this speaking likeness must be the portrait of the Count by Piero now in the Uffizi Gallery. Since the poem, now in the Vatican Library, was once in that of Urbino, it can be safely assumed that the Prince thus apostrophised is indeed Federico; but, if the portrait of him is that which is now in the Uffizi, it would seem that the Triumph on the reverse and the pendant portrait of the Countess, together with her Triumph, were added at a later date. It is not only that it would seem rather rude of the poet under the circumstances to have left the Countess out. There is internal evidence to suggest that her portrait and the Triumphs were painted during the next decade. Meanwhile, however, it is important to know that Piero had probably painted a portrait of Count Federico by 1466.

At the end of that year the painter is recorded at Arezzo. Had he only just finished the frescoes in S. Francesco? Or is this the time when he painted in fresco the single figure of *St Mary Magdalen* against the door of the Sacristy in Arezzo Cathedral? It only just escaped eclipse when a huge funeral monument was transferred to the same wall on the other side of it, so that it now looks sadly squeezed between the two. It would seem to have been painted later than *The Legend of the Holy Cross*, for there is a softness about the form which might well have been induced by the same feeling which led Piero finally to adopt the pure oil medium towards the end of his career. He has stood his young Magdalen in an arch of beautifully carved white stone, and has turned her scarlet mantle inside out over her shoulder to show the white lining symbolical of her mended ways. He treats her with gentle indulgence; indeed the appeal of her frailty is an interesting comment on all his other women. In the *Magdalen* the remoteness seems no more than a momentary abstraction. The line of her cheek and neck, purer than ever between the voluptuous lips and the curls of the slightly dishevelled hair, is no longer that of carved marble but of some exquisite vase turned in the soft clay. Piero has never let the light play more caressingly.

The record of his presence at Arezzo in 1466 concerns only a picture which must long ago have served its purpose and been thrown away, in spite of the care which he evidently devoted to it. This was a standard with *The Annunciation* painted on both sides for the Confraternity of that name. From the wording of the agreement signed on 20 December they appear to have tried to find a good and sufficient painter in Florence only to decide upon *Maestro Pietro di Benedetto dal Borgo Santo Sepolchro*, he who painted the *chupola maggiore* of S. Francesco in Arezzo. Perhaps their insistence that both Virgin and Archangel should have gentle and angelic countenances shows that the severity of Piero's style had caused them some qualms. They were probably wanting to be up-to-date when they stipulated that the medium should be oil. Piero intended to do the painting at Sansepolcro, where he was re-elected to the Council the following year. In 1468, in order to escape the plague, he moved with the canvas to the neighbouring village of Bastia; and it was here, on 7 November, that the Confraternity's Treasurer came with two of his colleagues to pay the balance to Piero and carry the standard off to Arezzo with a horse and cart. It is a relief to know that the remainder of the Company found it beautiful when it was borne before them on the following Sunday.* It was still in use in the time of Vasari.

This enforced move of Piero's to Bastia may explain why it was not until a year and a week after the delivery of the standard that he seems to have been able to hand over, finished, the great polyptych for the high altar of S. Agostino at Sansepolcro, of which the centrepiece is lost. When he had contracted to paint this, rather more than fourteen years earlier, he had promised delivery in eight years. The panels and almost certainly the frame had already been manufactured for him,

* G. Milanesi in *Giornale storico d. Archivi toscani*, VI, 1862, pp. 10–15; and *Scritti vari sulla Storia dell'Arte Toscana*, 1873, pp. 299–302.

and the long period stipulated for the painting was due presumably to the engagement not long undertaken to paint the fresco cycle at Arezzo. He was not to know that a summons from the Pope to Rome would make the interval still longer. A vivid fragment of fresco, with the head and one shoulder of *An unidentified young Saint (St Julian?)*, which is now in the Gallery at Sansepolcro, comes from the choir of S. Agostino; and it is puzzling if this once full-length fresco was painted there by Piero, as several excellent authorities believe, during these long years between the contract for the high altarpiece and its delivery. The style shows that it was certainly not painted after 1469, when the high altarpiece was probably set up. A justifiable solution is that it had been painted in or before 1454; for it is not difficult to find echoes of Andrea del Castagno in the pure fresco technique, in the sharp brilliance of the lighting and in the startled, frowning expression of the Saint.

We do not know that *The Legend of the Holy Cross* was completed much before 1466 (or even then); and, if several pictures on panel had been painted during the earlier 'sixties, as they would seem to have been, before Piero painted the Annunciation banner, these were comparatively small and probably the work of the winter months, when painting on wet plaster in an unheated church would have been disagreeable and unhealthy. This high altarpiece for S. Agostino, with five large compartments, and perhaps many small subsidiaries, was something on a new scale, the largest of Piero's recorded undertakings in tempera or oil; and it called for new methods of painting. It is not surprising that it was not completed earlier if the plague at Sansepolcro followed not long after he had put the finishing touches to the frescoes at Arezzo, when he must have been hoping for an interval in his studio at home. The four side panels of the main tier, each with a single figure, still exist, though they are dispersed among as many nations. Of the large central compartment the very theme is still legitimate matter for speculation, for the altrpiece was never described and a specification of all that was to be depicted on it has disappeared. We know of this from a reference in the contract, which itself has come down to us not in the original but in the form of a contemporary notary's copy. This, however, tells us so much about the customs of the period that it is perhaps worth attempting a translated précis of the Latin text, though this cannot be done without free interpretation. *

Dated 4 October 1454, the instrument describes a meeting of the Chapter of S. Agostino in the sacristy of the church. It was called by the Prior of the Monastery and was declared open 'at the sound of the bell which was rung three times according to custom'. Of the Chapter, the document states, there were present, besides the Prior, 'the pious man' Fra Francesco Nicolai of Borgo, of the Augustinian Order, and Fra Giuliano of Foligno 'reader and preacher', Fra Petrus Johannis and Fra Johannes Johannis of Germany, whose qualities go unspecified. Also present were 'the honourable men' Nannes Cischii and Ser Ughuccius Nofri of Luxembourg, '*operarii*' [surveyors?] of the church, Angelo di Giovanni di Simone d'Angelo of Borgo Sansepolcro, who was going to pay for the picture, and Piero di Benedetto di Pietro, who was to paint it. Also present was the altarpiece itself, unpainted and perhaps not yet gilt. It had been constructed at Angelo's expense, and, presumably, offered up on the high altar. It was evidently now in the sacristy and was thereby consigned to Piero 'for painting and decorating and gilding with

* Millard Meiss in *The Art Bulletin*, March 1941, pp. 53 ff.; he reproduces the documents.

those images, figures, pictures and ornaments' which had been separately particu-
larised and agreed upon in writing. Piero was to use 'good and fine colours and
gold and silver and other ornamentation'. Only the front was to be painted, and
the completed polyptych was to be set up on the high altar in eight years' time. The
contract was for 320 florins, of which Angelo was to pay down one hundred in
cash, together with a piece of arable land nearby which still had to be valued. When
the picture was ready, Angelo was to pay Piero another fifty florins plus any
balance remaining from the 320 after the valuation of the land. Angelo promised
all this not only of his own devotion but in fulfilment of the wishes of his deceased
brother Simone and of Simone's wife Johanna, not to mention the souls of their
ancestors. *

The receipt for a payment to Piero on 14 November 1469 is so complicated as
regards currency that it is impossible to deduce from it that both parties had now
discharged their obligations in full; but it undoubtedly refers to the picture as
painted. Not everybody agrees now that this payment represented the final settle-
ment; but then nobody knows on the other hand how promptly Angelo di
Giovanni was in the habit of paying up. In other words the date of completion is
not quite firm. That this great complex of pictures was finally placed on the high
altar of S. Agostino at Sansepolcro we know only from Vasari, who mentions it
there and states that it had been highly praised, in both the printed editions of his
Lives of 1550 and 1568. In fact, probably, it had been removed from the high altar
during the interval between the two editions. In 1555 the Augustinians lost their
church to the Poor Clares, who remodelled it and reconsecrated it as Sta Chiara.
The Augustinians acquired another church, the Pieve di Sta Maria; but this new
S. Agostino was totally rebuilt in 1773. If one of the panels was indeed in a Spanish
collection before the end of the eighteenth century (and, if one, probably two), it
cannot have been later than this that the altarpiece was broken up, some time before
the monastery was suppressed in 1808. The church became a concert hall. The
components of the altarpiece may have been scattered as early as 1555, for, while
the Clares set up a high-altarpiece of their own, some of the panels from the
pilasters or *predella* may have remained. Little pictures by Piero in the choir of
Sta Chiara are mentioned as late as 1832 in a guide to the art treasures of the
neighbourhood.† These can hardly have been frescoes, though there must have
been other frescoes there besides that which has partly survived.

These little pictures may well have included the three which are now in the
Washington National Gallery and in the Frick Collection, New York, for all three
represent Saints in half length on panels of the same size and shape with gold
grounds, and are thus likely to have come from the pilasters or the *predella* of a
great altarpiece. One of the two Saints in the Frick Collection wears the black habit
and leather belt of the Augustinian Friars, the other, dressed as a nun in black, has
been identified as St Augustine's mother, St Monica. St Apollonia in Washington,
wearing a rose mantle over a sky blue robe, is easily identified by the pincers in
which she holds one of her teeth, record of her death by cruel torture in ancient
Alexandria. All three have Piero's vivid characterisation.

* Martin Davies, *National Gallery Catalogues, The Earlier Italian Schools*, second edition, 1961, pp.
428–33, brings the story up to date and gives all the references.
† Giacomo Marcini, *Instruzione Storico-Pittorica . . . di Città di Castello*, 1832, II, p. 272.

The circumstances described in the contract are cause for deliberation about the very nature of art. Things must have been done in just the same way in Romanesque times; and yet even the secondary pictures which resulted from this commission are little less than revolutionary in vision, in expression, in technique. Piero seemed to have no options. Before he began to paint, all the subjects had been decided, the panels cut, the frame carved. After the great spaces that he had been able to create and fill with his own creatures at Arezzo, he might well have felt himself intolerably inhibited. Yet to look at his *St Michael* in the National Gallery, London, come down out of the blue infinity of heaven to show himself in the place of honour at the Virgin's right hand, is to experience an instantaneous liberation of the spirit. For all that they are folded, these white wings alone, between the different blues of open sky and cuirass close-moulded to the body, make for something more than gladness. Demonstrating that the powers of evil are nothing but a poor red-blooded snake, the Generalissimo of the Heavenly Host is the very spirit of release from their dead weight. His uniform is that of a Caesar, but until one has seen it one does not know what blue can bring about, how much of darkness it can disperse. Piero's blues, made mostly from azurite and lead white, like any other painter's, are yet different from any other blues. They are more blue here by contrast with the orange-brown and the gold; but the subtlety of their expressiveness is due to the behaviour of Piero's light, now revealing the supple modelling of the cuirass, now deeply absorbed in the stuff of the tunic where it shows below the thick gold plates, now sparkling in the sapphires set in these, now milkily reflecting, in the steel at the shoulders, the white clouds that are unseen by us as they pass over our heads. Where the muslin shirt shows on neck and sleeves, the lights and shadows play a game of hide-and-seek so delicate that our smile is ready for the scarlet pills of buttons profiled on the arms.

This liberation by light is a liberation in space. The low, delicately moulded parapet of white marble with its panels in soft colour only makes us more conscious of the infinity beyond, and equally of the value of the light-filled space before it in which the Archangel stands. Space is not space without form, and live form is potential movement. St Michael balances on the serpent's body as one who has weight, but also wings. The grip of the hands, the tautness of wrists and arms express the same firm, stern, otherworldly resolution as the face.

To look back in time to the *St Michael* painted in fresco by Spinello Aretino on the wall of the nave of S. Francesco at Arezzo, which Piero surely had in mind when he painted this panel, for one holds a distinct echo of the other, is to realise that it is easier for the painter whose sense of form is not too strong to represent the supernatural in abstraction. Spinello's angular Archangel is a brightly spiritual conception which one is bound to admire; but his physical existence is not established convincingly. He has no space. Piero's Archangel appears to us in form quite as substantial as that of any of the other three figures on the same scale, which are earthbound. His spiritual detachment, his power to levitate are the result of indescribable subtleties of form and colour and light. The final refinement of the sense of form has to be expressed in the handling of the paint itself, for this is what distinguishes the quality of all the surfaces, in the very process of identifying texture and colour and light and form as one.

If Piero ever made a drawing for this picture it was but a vague one. He built it up as he went along, from back to front, making big changes in the position of the wings, painting the parapet before he painted the hand, painting the hand before the serpent's head, the serpent's head before the sword. One knows these things because the aged paint has grown transparent. The medium is no longer tempera, and not yet oil; it is shown by analysis to be an emulsion of the two. The colour is laid on as if it were oil paint, sometimes as freely as this was to be applied in the next century. For the most part the brush is not a fine one and its strokes are fused together; but where impasto is needed for the high-lights it may be applied with the finest of flicks, as in the lights of the jewels, or in a bold, straight stroke an inch long, as in the kink of the gold straps hanging from the shoulders. At the shoulders themselves the reflections from the steel might have been painted by a sixteenth-century Venetian.

The Chief Angel would naturally be given pride of place on the Virgin's right – on the left hand of the lost centrepiece – in deference to Angelo, the donor of the altarpiece; but the recent removal of overpaintings during the cleaning of the picture has made the fact visible. Two steps overlap from the larger panel into the bottom right corner of this one. The lower step, porphyry-coloured, reaches beyond the tip of St Michael's scarlet boot. The upper is entirely covered by heavy folds of gold and crimson damask, presumably the end of the Virgin's mantle; and above this the broken remains of a blue drapery hang in front of the parapet down the picture's right edge. The fact that these stuffs were so far to the side of the lost central compartment makes it very unlikely that this contained only a single Madonna enthroned in its centre. It gives support to the thesis already advanced from brilliant deductions by Mirella Levi d'Ancona* that the theme was 'The Coronation of the Virgin'.

The Frick Collection has the panel with *St Simon Zelotes*(?) which is shown by its counterpart of a more abrupt overlapping of steps to have adjoined *The Corona-tion*(?) on the other side. Both Angelo's dead brother, mentioned in the contract as a, so-to-speak, posthumous co-donor of the altarpiece, and their grandfather were called Simon; and this latterday convert among the Apostles is represented in his rare appearances in art as an old man with a white beard. Their father was Giovanni; and St John Evangelist, whose presence would have been more pleasing to the Friars, does seem to appear as a whitebeard in the last of Piero's great altar-pieces, now in the Brera Gallery, though he is usually represented in his youth. So there are two candidates for identification in this splendid head, which is, as Millard Meiss has pointed out, the head of King Solomon from Arezzo in reverse. Whatever his identity, this aged Apostle is the perfect counterpart to the eternal youth of the Archangel. Near to the end of his terrestrial life, with hair like white coral bristling on the skin like tanned leather covering his worn head, his hands and feet gnarled like the limbs of some rugged oak, he is firmly planted on the marble floor. The great mantle of deep crimson into which his withered body is withdrawn is a sculptured monolith, of which the wide curve on the outer side may well have echoed the movement of Christ in the central scene as he bent to place the Virgin's crown. There is a suggestion of blue from the azure sky in the high-lights on the crimson stuff; but the day is quite absorbed into the deep folds, as is the mind of the Apostle in the book over which he bends his head. To the

* See her *Supplement*, 1955, pp. 61 ff., to the large *Catalogue of the Frick Collection*.

gleam of the mounts on its green leather binding or to the glitter of the jewels on the golden border at the hem of his deep blue robe he is indifferent. These are concessions to us.

The *St Augustine* from the extreme left is now in Lisbon. As befits the Patron Saint, he is represented with most elaboration. Yet the wealth of ornament is the more severely contained within the cylindrical, near-symmetrical outline of mitre and cope. Beneath him we are looking for the first time at a floor-space unencumbered by intrusion from *The Coronation*(?) scene, and the outlines of the form which almost covers it describe a section like that of some great Gothic pier rising to support the roof of a cathedral. The slim and fragile crozier of crystal makes a perfect foil to this density and weight, emphasising by its absolute verticality the almost straightness of the columns of drapery, relieving their deep chiaroscuro by its translucency, acting as a light-conductor from earth to ether, relaxing in a joyous curl as it escapes to send out messages of light. This is the richest panel of them all in its harmony of now melting now contrasted colour-and-light; and Piero, not content with the splendid figure in gold thread upon the deep blue ground of the damask and its heavy gold fringe, has edged the cope with a wide orphrey of embroidered scenes. On the mitre itself Christ at full length shows his Cross and wounds above a row of half-length Martyrs, and on the great brooch below he rises from the tomb. On the orphrey at the neck are four Saints, with Peter and Paul conspicuous on the right shoulder. Below these the New Testament history begins with the Annunciation. We can see no further than the Crucifixion on the other side. As the cope is pulled outwards by the Saint's arms, to slant very slightly inwards again towards the hem at the foot, these little scenes are brilliantly foreshortened. Ingeniously, this enhances the drama of the themes, so broadly composed that we can read each one of them. It is Piero's consummate control of form and knowledge of tone-values which enable him to brush in these scenes in so remarkable a mixture of vagueness and clarity. One is reminded less of the Venetians, who first learned from Piero this art of sheer painting, than of those little fingernail sketches of Philip IV and his courtiers by Velazquez in the *Boar Hunt* of the London National Gallery. The *St Augustine* seems to have escaped the ruthless scrubbing which has at some time worn much of the surface from the *St Michael*, and one cannot appreciate so well in any other picture the joyous touches without number which suggest the very weight and structure of every detail in all this elaborate ornamentation. Yet it does not overlay the power and character of the forms. That hand grasping the translucent rod is turned by the white glove into a piece of pure sculpture, lovely in itself, but underlining the resolution in the ardent, intellectual face.

Originally at the other end of the altarpiece, on the extreme right, *St Nicholas of Tolentino* is now in the Poldi-Pezzoli Museum in Milan. Again, the contrast could hardly be stronger. S. Agostino, the greatest of the Latin Fathers of the Church, dead more than a thousand years, is idealised in every way. St Nicholas, a favourite Augustinian Saint, canonised only in 1446, is treated as a contemporary might be. But for the halo and the star which shone over Tolentino at his birth, we might be looking at the first of full-length portraits in anything but the name. The probability is that we are, and it is difficult not to ask whether we do not have before us the Prior of S. Agostino at Sansepolcro. It would have been tactless, surely, to portray anyone else who might be recognised there. Certainly this powerful man would make the perfect Prior. He is not given to the emotional oratory of a St Bernardino. He advises us shrewdly, though not unkindly, out of long experience of all the sorts that it took to make the world of the Renaissance. He is a firm administrator, and his solid bulk is a guarantee of his humanity. It is a superb bulk, leaving us in no doubt of the extent of its displacement or of the body structure beneath the black Augustinian habit. To let one's eye travel from the edge of the dark grey sleeve at the wrist to the top of the black hood from which the great head emerges is to be exhilarated vicariously by a mountain climb. The third edition of Longhi's book has a detail in colour of the left arm and hand holding the great blue-bound tome at an angle to the stout column habited in black. As one looks at the hand emerging from the hollow of the sleeve and above it through the deep cave, with its slanting floor of book, to the blue sky beyond, one has such a sensation as one experiences from the sculptured cavities of some great 'Reclining Figure' by Henry Moore.

These four monumental panels, with all their richness and variety, are but subsidiaries, intended to minister by their harmonies and their arrangement to the great composition which they originally served as wings. By their consummate mastery of form and of the technique of painting they tell us that in this *Coronation of the Virgin*(?) we have lost one of the great painted masterpieces of all time.

To close this chapter of masterpieces with the complex of pictures forming the altarpiece at Perugia and the other complex of problems which goes with it is something of an anticlimax. Nevertheless, it is easier to evaluate it satisfactorily at this point, after the story has been told of how the great polyptych for S. Agostino was commissioned and some attempt made to describe the breadth and freedom of Piero's work at the end of the decade of the 'sixties, when he himself was probably some sixty years old. The conditions which he had had to accept in 1454, when he was already working at Arezzo, do much to explain by analogy what first needs explanation in the Perugia altarpiece: its provincial character as a piece of furniture. This commission, too, he may have accepted many years before; but such an explanation is perhaps unnecessary at this moment, even if the frescoes at Arezzo had made his name known beyond the boundaries of Southern Tuscany and Umbria. There was little employment for painters in Rome under the immediate successors to Pius II, and the fierce competition among artists in Florence is unlikely to have appealed to Piero's temperament. Perugia was once his capital and was always very near his home; and, if the nuns of S. Antonio there had ideas about painting which were boring to a man of his inventiveness and intellectual resources, Piero must by this time have been under the necessity of finding employment for pupils. It is not surprising therefore to discover what a comparison with the S. Agostino panels makes plain: that in the Perugia altarpiece Piero himself did a limited amount of the actual painting, even – perhaps least of all – in the main tier.

This part, which forms a triptych with the enthroned *Madonna* in the centre and, as in the *Misericordia* polyptych of Piero's earliest days, a pair of Saints, *SS. Anthony of Padua and John Baptist, SS. Francis and Elizabeth of Hungary* in each of the two wings, is enclosed in what is said to be its original frame. This is modest enough, and softly carved; but it is topped by Gothic arches with a restless array of

64

cusps below and florid combing above. Still more embarrassing to the painter must have been the gilded grounds of the panels, damascened in one bold pattern for the centre and another for those on either side. No barest chance of suggesting infinity here. The framing of the parts above and below dates from after 1810, when the altarpiece had been moved from S. Antonio delle Monache at Perugia to the National Gallery for Umbria there. It had been previously dismembered. In the reconstruction the whole was made to look ill-proportioned and cumbersome by the insertion, between the main tier and the *predella* with its three painted scenes, of an inappropriate upper *predella* tier. This is said to be on one piece of wood; but the painting is modern except for the two little roundels and some ornamentation to one side of each. This is very similar to ornament in *The Annunciation* which, over the main tier, completes the altarpiece in one wide scene at the top. In the roundels are painted against a black ground two little half-length figures: *St Clare*(?) and *St Agatha*, the latter easily identified by the little breasts which she offers cheerfully like sweetmeats upon a silver dish.

The crowning awkwardness of the whole is the present shape of *The Annunciation*. It has been cut brutally at the sides into angles which are equally incompatible with the soft curves of the original frame below it and with the composition of the painting, now edged by a meagre baguette. The panel must have been reduced also along the foot, for the framing of *The Madonna* below now intrudes into the foreground of *The Annunciation*, cutting away the pedestal intended to support the twin columns to the left of the Virgin Annunciate. Thus the very crux of the architectural design is gone, there is no support where support is most of all essential, and the position of the Virgin Annunciate is made to seem ambiguous. Such fundamental errors are unthinkable in any picture composed by Piero. Once we assume, however, that they were not there originally, no deficiencies in the execution of this picture can make it less than one of his happiest designs.

By a lucky chance, Vasari, who in his second edition, of 1568, is the first to report the existence of the altarpiece, in this case went to the trouble of recording its subjects and their arrangement:

> In the church of the ladies of St Anthony of Padua, in a tempera panel, Our Lady with her Son on her lap, St Francis, St Elizabeth, St John Baptist and St Anthony of Padua; and over this the most beautiful Annunciation, with an angel who really seems to have come from heaven, and, what is more, a perspective of diminishing columns, beautifully done. In the *predella* . . . St Anthony bringing a boy back to life, St Elizabeth saving a child fallen into a well, and St Francis receiving the stigmata.

Thus we know that a century or less after the altarpiece was painted it was topped by *The Annunciation*; and the possibility, which has been often mooted, that *The Annunciation* was once of significantly different shape or in quite another place seems to be minimal. The most recent proposition on these lines, made by C. L. Ragghianti,* that this was originally a separate altarpiece, rectangular in shape and at least twice as big in area, postulates in the first place the barbarous mutilation during the Renaissance of a thoroughly Renaissance picture in order to hoist the remnant of it over an altarpiece in a Gothic frame which was itself much less fashionable in design. It ignores the fact that the perspective is planned to be seen

---

* See Del Buono and De' Vecchi, *L'Opera completa di Piero della Francesca*, 1967, pp. 102–3.

XXVI. *The Resurrection*, fresco 225 × 200 cms. Palazzo Comunale, Sansepolcro
XXVII. (Overleaf) detail from *The Resurrection*, figures in central foreground
XXVIII. Detail from *The Resurrection*, figures in right foreground

XXVIII

XXX

from below, much as it is now. Moreover the resulting composition, however fascinating to mathematicians, is very cumbersome, and quite overwhelms the figures by the architecture. It seems more in accordance both with the one record that we have and with the architectural probabilities, within the picture and without, that the altarpiece was designed for a comparatively small chapel; that *The Annunciation* which was its culmination had to fit under a curved vault; that it was originally deeper at the foot and therefore cut much less or not at all there by the frame of the centre panel; that its peak was the culmination of sides which originally were curved, as in any other Gothic design and in accordance with the lines of the postulated vault. Such a curve would have accommodated all the architecture in the picture without its being chopped and distorted as it is now, and would give considerably more expression to the attitudes of the Virgin and the Angel.

No doubt the nuns of S. Antonio had wanted such an altarpiece as Fra Angelico, more than thirty years before, had painted for the friars of S. Domenico (this now faces Piero's altarpiece in the Perugia Gallery). Here too the centre panel with the Madonna, seated on a throne forming a tall niche above her in order to fill its greater height, is flanked on either side by a shorter panel of equal width with two Saints partly separated by the cusp of the twin-arched top. Unfortunately, Angelico's triptych has been reframed entirely; but there can be no doubt that his two painted roundels, with the separate figures of Gabriel and the Virgin together forming an *Annunciation*, were originally sited as they are in the new frame, over the cusp on each of the wings. The nuns having decided to go one better than the friars, and to have their *Annunciation* in an elaborate scene over the whole triptych, there would have been a need for two other subjects for roundels in their altarpiece. Piero's roundels with *St Clare*(?) and *St Agatha*, not mentioned by Vasari, would have fitted nicely and less conspicuously here; and the decoration attached to them would have been in closer relationship to its counterpart in the architecture of *The Annunciation*.

In designing his only enthroned Madonna – for no other unaccompanied Madonna by him has come down to us either in substance or in record – Piero was still haunted by the memory of Masaccio's Madonna at Pisa, painted half a century before. Once again the Virgin leans her powerful frame forward from the throne as if to protect the Child, who once again squeezes grapes in his powerful little fist. But Piero was not Pieraccio, and his equally powerful Christ Child has already accepted with a good will the duties of his Ministry. As in the Sinigallia picture, he sits upright to bestow his blessing, with grave benevolence. He wears no domestic coral here, nor any garment. His Mother has the same homely head-dress; but the nuns have insisted upon haloes, which are worn throughout the altarpiece. Thick discs of gold, highly polished, they are drawn in perspective and, like those in the later of the two panels of the *Misericordia* polyptych, reflect all too clearly the tops of the heads beneath them. The upper part of this picture, the hood of the throne, the head and breast of the Virgin, the Child, are painted freely, in emulsion probably, or in oils, evidently by Piero himself. The Virgin's mantle, of ultramarine apparently, is perhaps the most intense blue that Piero ever used. In the remainder of the principal tier the figures are sculptural as ever, but they are tamely painted and, for all the deep rose of St John Baptist's mantle and the crimson of St Anthony's book, the colour is somewhat drab and monochrome and badly

XXIX. (Previous page) detail from *The Madonna and Child with Two Angels*, head of the Virgin, panel 61 × 53.5 cms. Galleria Nazionale delle Marche, Urbino
XXX. Detail from *The Madonna and Child with Two Angels*, the Christ Child

balanced as between wing and wing. Above all, the sense of space which Piero has taught us to expect is lacking. Allowance must be made, however, for the condition of the paint, especially in the right panel. It is not very good, and the partial cleaning and restoration, done in 1951, seem to have included the putting back of some of the discoloration from the old varnish in the new. This mélange helps to conceal damages and preserves the effect of mellowed ageing which is often admired in pictures, as it is in furniture; but it obscures the quality of the painting.

Perhaps the same treatment of the surface is the cause of a certain tameness in the colouring of *The Annunciation*. The dull unvaried pink of the large flags in the foreground pavement and of the entire floor of the cloister beyond, * the almost identical blues of Gabriel's tunic and wings, of the marble panel at the end of the arcade and of the sky itself do not sing with the clarity or the modulation of tone which give such vitality to the frescoes at Arezzo or the three pictures in the London National Gallery now that these have been cleaned. The apparently jet black panel behind the Virgin seems opposed to Piero's principle of infinity, and the porphyry between the twin columns even seems difficult to explain. It goes against the grain, however, to cavil at what is still, even in its mutilated condition, one of Piero's stupendous achievements. Here too he can hardly have begun his design without remembering Masaccio's prototype, *The Annunciation* now lost from S. Niccoló in Florence 'with a house and many columns, admirably painted', Vasari assures us, 'in perspective . . . the whole . . . so managed that the colonnade gradually recedes from view in a manner which proves Masaccio's knowledge of perspective'. Piero's cloister, with its loggia for the Virgin's readings brought forward to one side and its enclosed garden on the other, is the most serenely sumptuous of all the architectural dreams which painters have bequeathed to us. Mathematics and colour consummate their marriage in a shimmering ecstasy of cool light, and gaily dare us to tread with our dusty feet in these shapely spaces, which surely exist but are radiant and pure beyond our mundane experience. It is doubtful if a brush in any hand but Piero's could have managed that delicate infinity of white capitals and entablatures in which the dancing of the light reaches such dizzy speed, after the slower measures upon the floor below and the quickening of contrasts in the vault. Certainly Piero alone can have painted the upper part of the Archangel, who is one of the noblest of his Arcadians, or the tree behind him, which is the tree of the Urbino *Allegory* brought to a closer view.

Though much damaged, the three little scenes of the *predella* seem to be widely accepted now as Piero's own work. This must be correct; they are so effectively dramatic, so boldly conceived in terms of space and light and shade, so broadly, almost casually painted. *St Anthony resuscitates a Dead Baby* on the left is an unforgettable drama of domestic humanity within four walls. *The Stigmatisation of St Francis*, helped perhaps by the memory of Spinello's imposing nocturne in fresco in S. Francesco at Arezzo, is terrible for the loneliness of the bare hill-side at night. In the main tier St Francis shows hands that are not just pierced symbolically but maimed by the very agony of the Cross. In this *predella* scene the scarlet vision in the blue-black sky diffuses a warmly comforting radiance over the rocks.

---

* There may, however, be evidence here that *The Annunciation* was painted at Perugia. I am not familiar with the building materials used there in the fifteenth century; but the great hall of the palace which houses the National Gallery for Umbria is now paved with a marble of this colour.

10 · The Urbino Triumphs

In the early Spring of 1469, some months before he received what was probably the final payment for the S. Agostino altarpiece at Sansepolcro, Piero had paid a visit to Urbino. There he was put up by the young painter and poet Giovanni Santi, who fourteen years later was to become the father of Raphael. For the modest expenses thus incurred Santi was reimbursed on 8 April by the Confraternity of the Corpus Domini, who had invited Piero to come and estimate for painting their large altarpiece with *The Communion of the Apostles*. It is in their records that he 'had come to see the panel with a view to painting it' (*chera venuto a vedere la taula per farla*).* The *predella* for this wide panel, now in the Palace at Urbino, had already been painted, some two years before, by Uccello and it is generally supposed that the Florentine had also made a design for the main panel, which had been rejected. If so, this cannot have been altogether unexpected by those who knew Uccello's work – and he was now near to the end of his long career. It would be indecent to compare the six scenes on one long plank in which he illustrates an anti-Semitic story called *The Profanation of the Host* with a strip cartoon; but the sceptical humour of their racy narrative is one of the charms of these beautiful and scientifically designed little pictures.

It seems much more surprising that nothing came of it when Piero gave his consideration to the equally unusual theme of the main picture. He may have accepted the commission. Indeed, he may even have begun the painting, though we know only that a frame was made for the panel in the winter of 1470–71, and that Piero was probably away from Sansepolcro at this time: his name was posted there in February 1471 among those who had not yet paid their taxes. And yet it was a Netherlandish painter, Joos van Wassenhove, identified in the Urbino documents as *Giusto da Guanto*, Justus of Ghent, who came to paint the great *Communion of the Apostles*, now also in the Palace at Urbino. Something which happened in the meantime must have diverted Piero and the Confraternity from the original intention. Perhaps it was the death of the Countess Battista, Federico's second wife, on 6 July 1472.

The instalments paid to Justus began only in February 1473. On 7 March 1474 fifteen gold florins were contributed by Federico. Justus had included him in the picture, together with the two things of which he was most proud. He appears behind the circle of Apostles in conversation with the Persian Ambassador to his court, while his son and heir, the infant Guidobaldo, born in January 1472, is brought on in the arms of his nurse. Battista had died soon after bringing him into the world. The baby's age in the picture suggests that this must have been begun about the end of 1472. Chronology is of some importance here because it may give the answer to two questions of varying importance: why did Piero not paint the Corpus Domini altarpiece; when did he paint the companion *Portraits of Count*

* Jacques Lavallaye, *Le Palais Ducal d'Urbin*, 1964, pp. 1–40, including new documents (pp. 31–36).

Federico and Countess Battista which are now in the Uffizi Gallery (they were brought to Florence from Urbino in 1631).

It is relevant also to note that the Company of the Corpus Domini would seem to have been the first to give a commission to Justus. We do not therefore have to accept as gospel the statement of Vespasiano da Bisticci in his life of Federico, to whom he was for a time librarian, that the Count had actually sent to the Netherlands in search of '*un maestro solenne*' who could paint on panel in oils. It is true that Justus is recorded at Ghent as late as 1469, but he may have arrived at Urbino after a visit to Rome, whither another Ghent record of a few years later states that he had gone. Federico, however, may have brought him from there. Very little went on at Urbino without his knowledge, and he had probably been in the confidence of the Confraternity from the beginning concerning their anxiety over their altarpiece. No doubt Uccello's design for it, with the *predella*, led to the insistence of all parties on the painter's solemnity, a word that the biographer uses more than once. What is more important, the death of the Countess Battista in July 1472, if it was followed by the commission from her bereaved husband to Piero for the Uffizi portraits, absolves us from having to believe Vespasiano's implication that Federico preferred Justus to all the Italian painters, of whom he might have had virtually the pick. Certainly he proceeded to put Justus in charge of the decoration of his sumptuously panelled little study with the series of *Portraits of Illustrious Men* which is now divided between the Palace at Urbino and the Louvre; and certainly his confidence was justified. In *The Communion of the Apostles*, Justus' first attempt to design on the larger scale of Italy resulted in a somewhat eccentric composition; but of the twenty-eight *Portraits* those which can confidently be attributed to him include some of the noblest of the many attempts by Renaissance painters to portray ideal men. Those by the Spaniard Berruguete, who worked in the studio of Justus at Urbino, are notably less solemn. Over these works, however, the two portraits now in the Uffizi Gallery would plainly have had precedence, and Piero took a long time over every picture. Not only were the two portraits subjects of the utmost care; each has a *Triumph* of the sitter on the reverse.

The resulting ensemble has been described by John Pope-Hennessy as 'one of the great monuments of ruler portraiture'. Indeed, with his genius for symbolism Piero has made it seem that it is the world which is the less important thing, behind and far below these two imposing profiles; and the *Triumphs* leave us in no doubt. These have that supreme intensity in conception and in execution which had characterised the *Allegory with the Flagellation*. If Battista sat to Piero for this portrait, then both could have been painted much earlier than I am supposing. An argument over their date has gone on for many years; but Pope-Hennessy's pronouncement, the most recent to come from an authoritative source, seems to have been made with an unaccustomed brevity of consideration. He states 'It is established by A. Cinquini that the panels were in existence in 1466, when a poem on them was written by the Carmelite Ferabos. The poem reads: IMAGO EJUSDEM PRINCIPIS A PIETRO BURGENSI PICTA ALLOQUITUR IPSUM PRINCIPEM ... (THE LIKENESS OF THE PRINCE PAINTED BY PIERO DELLA FRANCESCA ADDRESSES THE PRINCE HIMSELF).' Pope-Hennessy goes on to translate the whole poem; but this tells us no more than its title, the crux being in the four last bathetic lines: 'Piero has given me nerves and flesh and bone / But thou, Prince, hast supplied me with a soul from thy divinity. / Therefore, I live, and speak and have movement of myself. / Thus does the glory of the King transcend the glory of the artist.' Is this really enough to *establish* the fact that Ferabò had seen *two* portraits which share a continuous landscape background and were always framed more or less as one, to say nothing of the scintillating *Triumphs* on their reverses? Is the known presence of Ferabò at Urbino in 1465–6 enough to prove that his poem was written then and not later? Pope-Hennessy continues: 'An attempt of C. E. Gilbert to date the panels after the death of Battista Sforza on 6 July 1472, is unconvincing.'* The evidence identifying the single portrait of Federico mentioned by Ferabò with a part of this complex of four pictures rests on nothing but the absence of any other portrait of the Count by Piero today, and it is worth examining once more the clues provided by the portraits themselves.

First there are the two Latin inscriptions in Sapphic verse under the *Triumphs* depicted on the reverses. Engraved in the same beautiful Roman lettering as the signature on the *Allegory with the Flagellation*, they read (under Federico's *Triumph*):

CLARVS INSIGNI VEHITVR TRIVMPHO / QVEM PAREM SVMMIS DVCIBVS PER-HENNIS / FAMA VIRTVTVM CELEBRAT DECENTER / SCEPTRA TENENTEM

and (under Battista's *Triumph*):

QVE MODVM REBVS TENVIT SECVNDIS / CONIVGIS MAGNI DECORATA RERVM / LAVDE GESTARVM VOLITAT PER ORA / CVNCTA VIRORVM

Many translations have been made into Italian, English and German, but all have been made in the context of the pictures, and have been therefore biased, consciously or unconsciously, by the need for compatibility with their accredited history. Appealed to in 1967 for a literal translation, but not informed of the origin or context of the verses or of any controversy over their meaning, Colin Haycraft kindly rendered them into English thus: 'He rides illustrious in glorious triumph – he whom, as he wields the sceptre with moderation, the eternal fame of his virtues celebrates as equal to the greatest generals'; and 'She who observed restraint in success flies on all men's lips honoured by the praise of her great husband's exploits.' Haycraft has clearly felt the distinction of sense and tenses: the present for Federico, for Battista the past.

Next among the clues is the apparent age of the sitters. When the couple were married in 1459 – one of the two moments when such a pair of portraits is most likely to have been painted – Battista was at most fourteen years of age. Even in 1466 she was not more than twenty-one. At the time of her death in 1472, though the mother of nine children, she was about twenty-seven. This seems the age most compatible with her profile in the portrait, which might very well have been done, like many other portraits of the Renaissance, from a death-mask. Among others Clark, while accepting the date of 1465 as almost certain, remarks on the lifeless expression: 'her eye little more than a conventional symbol'.†

Battista, daughter of Alessandro Sforza, Lord of Pesaro, was also the daughter

* John Pope-Hennessy, *The Portrait in the Renaissance*, 1966, p. 319, note 8; A. Cinquini in *L'Arte*, IX, 1906, p. 56; C.E. Gilbert in *Marsyas*, I, 1941, pp. 41–51.
† Clark, *op. cit.*, p. 39.

and grand-daughter of highly literate women. Her mother died while she was a baby, and she cannot be said to have had a childhood. Yet she survived the fearsome education to which, like many princesses of the Renaissance, she was subjected, to earn a great reputation not only for devoutness and modesty but for political tact and judgment. Pius II thought that her renown should have been greater than it was. At the age of fourteen she found herself a mother, and thereafter quite often virtually the regent, while her husband was abroad on a campaign. They had a second palace at Gubbio, over the crest of the Apennines to the west, where Federico had been born; and it was to this home that he had to ride day and night when he heard that Battista was dying, arriving only in time to close her eyes.

Federico had been enjoying a triumph in Florence, having waged a successful campaign on that state's behalf. He was indeed now at the zenith of his career. His many victories, sometimes almost as much diplomatic as military, had brought to Italy a momentary peace and to himself the respect of all the great powers. He had enlarged his own dominions, mainly at the expense of Malatesta, whom he now with prudent generosity had to protect from extinction. His palace at Urbino had by this time taken the essentials of its noble form under his eyes, though they were still carving the detail in the Court of Honour when Laurana departed in 1472. A happy marriage, which had so far resulted only in eight daughters, had at last been crowned by the birth of a son and heir. The death of his undoubtedly beloved wife was thus made all the more crushing by the irony of its timing. His real anguish rings out through the pompous verbiage in which he announced his loss to the heads of the various states, who proceeded to load him with honours in their attempts at consolation. Pope Sixtus IV made him Duke of Urbino with prodigious ceremony in 1474. Federico must have had good warning, and it is not impossible that the word *ducibus* introduced under his *Triumph* had a special meaning.

At the time of his wife's death he was some fifty years old. In a portrait painted after it one might expect to find him looking rather older than he does in the Uffizi portrait. He had begun his career as a soldier before he succeeded to Urbino in 1444, and not long after his succession he had lost his right eye and part of his nose in an ill-omened tournament. In the course of his subsequent campaigns he had suffered many injuries and occasional bouts of illness. His way of life was frugal, but extremely strenuous. However, if at this juncture Battista's likeness could have been made only from a death-mask, Federico's might equally well have been taken by Piero from a portrait painted at an earlier date. It is not impossible even that he now worked over his portrait of Federico which Ferabò appears to have seen. While the profile of the Countess is carved with unwavering directness, that of the Count shows at least one obvious alteration in the thickening of the neck – the other changes would be relatively superficial. True to his idea of unity, Piero has posed both his sitters in the same light. Coming from behind her husband, the sun falls full upon Battista's face, its light unscattered, as if diffused over a surface smooth as wax, which is all that Piero may have had before him as he painted. Indeed, this would explain a certain difficulty he seems to have had in uniting head and neck. Under the much yellowed varnish there is a brighter tone and more colour in the flesh than we can see now; or there would be too much

incongruity between the waxen head and the rich, soft, sensuous modelling of the
braided hair, with its entwined ribands and that intricately sculptured bundle of
white lawn. The jewellery, which by all accounts Battista had rarely taken from
her casket except to please her lord, seems now to be exulting in a permanent
licence to receive the attentions of the sun. In contrast with the deep blue damask
of the dress the sleeve is a blaze of gold brocade, figured in red and quilted.
Federico, in contrast, is unadorned and clad severely in uniform scarlet, whereas
in the many other portraits he is dressed with the utmost richness. There must be a
reason for this abnormality. Is it also a part of Piero's symbolism that he arranged
for Federico's features to be cast in shadow? It may only be that the half-light
allowed him better opportunity to chisel out a telling description of their rugged,
inviolable strength. It was not only emulation of the coins and medals of Antiquity
which made the profile the fashionable view in the portraits of the early Renaissance.
It is from the side that the permanent and fundamental characteristics of expression
are revealed most clearly.

The consistency of the lighting in these two portraits, while it distinguishes, also,
as always, unifies; and the continuity of the landscape behind the couple leaves us
in no doubt that in the Audience Chamber(?) at Urbino the two panels were
framed at least as close together as they are now, perhaps closer, with only the
slenderest of pillarets between them, as if they were seen together through a little
colonnade formed by the frame. The sitters are posed vertiginously high above the
landscape in a way which is itself an allegory. Behind the profile of the Count, or
Duke, Piero has used the wide waterway as a mirror to the sky, in order to enrich
and further unify the almost overwhelming effect of light-filled space. In this, with
his characteristic directness of idea, he has related the solemn pair to nature in a
manner which makes them a monument to man's capacity for exaltation. Their
profiles against the sky are immortalised with grave objectivity. We observe that
Oliver Cromwell was not the first of soldier-statesmen to insist upon the inclusion
of his warts. But nor was Federico, by any means. What was an exception in the
seventeenth century was the rule in the fifteenth. Early Renaissance man valued the
truth of appearances, and closed his eyes unwillingly to nature's characterisations.

The flattery is on the reverse, where in miniature each, as in the commemorative
medals of Antiquity, is the subject of a *Triumph*. From the beginning Piero's
imagery has rarely failed to suggest a significance coming from so far beneath the
surface of appearances that he may be said to have been painting allegories all his
life. Now that two allegories are his commissioned subject, the genius of his
invention is plain for all to see.

The inscriptions are engraved in the marble of a containing wall with plinth and
cornice carved to Greek perfection; so that our eye lights easily on the terrace of
levelled rock beyond, high above the misty panorama. Here in the pure light hero
and heroine are drawn to meet each other, enthroned on the two floats of Fortune
and Chastity. Their meeting is inevitable, for it is Love who guides each simple
car, needing neither rein nor bridle. White stallions snort as they draw that of
Fortune, who in her white shift balances confidently on her blue ball to fix the
Duce's crown. Federico, his right eye miraculously restored, sits in shining armour
with cloak and shoes of crimson, extending his baton over the heads of the four
Cardinal Virtues seated with legs dangling on the red carpet at his feet. Behind

the drab but excited unicorns of Chastity, Battista, attended by her duenna(?), is like a Virgin of the Annunciation, eyes lowered upon the book in her lap, with Hope beside her and Faith and Charity below. The part which they all are playing is in history, not in a pageant. No pageant could be so moving in its mixture of grandeur and simplicity; and the figures which compose it, historic and allegorical alike, are immersed in the sunlight which will soon be bathing the world below them. They exist in the ground, solid and tangible as little figures have been seen until now only in pictures from the Netherlands, by a Van Eyck or a Robert Campin.

In *The Triumphs*, as in *The Portraits*, the scenery is continuous; and these two wide landscapes, back and front, are unique. As panoramas they have a more opulent prototype in the view through the arches of Van Eyck's *Madonna of Chancellor Rollin* in the Louvre, one more passionate in those vistas of the Arno valley which the Pollaiuoli were painting in Florence; and already, in Venice or Padua, Giovanni Bellini must have painted that wide scene with *The Agony in the Garden* now in the London National Gallery, where the dawn landscape is as expressive as the *dramatis personae* themselves. Yet each of these scenes appears to be bound within the limits of its own nostalgia when we turn to look at this remoter world which Piero has dared to create out of sluggish water, out of farmland slopes, patterned and dotted haphazardly with hedge and shrub, and a distance of pimple-hills befogged in monochrome. In place of the varied fascination of all their detail and their emotional overtones, here is only an empty sky and the almost abstract music of measured intervals between gently sloping pyramids. Beneath them the half-seen plain is serenely waiting upon the sun. High above them, the Select are already triumphing in its brilliance. Cunningly, Piero has used a natural effect to bring our eye at once to hero and heroine, leaving the landscape to come slowly into shape out of its own infinity. More than any other landscape, this is in one sense a background; we are left in no doubt as to what is the proper study of mankind. But no picture was ever painted in which forms so near and immediate and forms so distant and eternal were yet convincingly united in the total harmony of light.

These landscapes are another reason for dating the four pictures as late as possible in the painter's career, for some of their features are found only in *The Nativity*, which has been widely accepted as one of his last works. The link is not only in their more distant forms, though these are noticeably similar (and Piero has carried over into *The Nativity* the idea of this vertiginous drop from foreground into middle distance by which the figures are made absolute), but in the quality which all the forms derive from the method of painting. There is enough of the original surface left in *The Nativity* to show that once it was like that of the Uffizi pictures. This is different from the surface of the *Allegory with the Flagellation*, which I have tried to show good reason for dating at least no earlier than the second half of the 'sixties. That is typical of the tempera medium. This is fused and richly oleaginous, in spite of the green copper resinate glazes which have gone brown – no doubt it was the belief that similar glazes were nothing but browned varnish which led to the scouring of *The Nativity*. Analysis by gas chromotography has shown that *The Nativity* was painted in oils; so that there need be little hesitation in accepting the fact that the paint on these four panels is what it seems: pure oil paint. The technique of all four pictures thus provides a final reason for dating them at least after 1469; for the S. Agostino altarpiece, which was delivered in that year, is known by analysis of the medium used in two of the panels, the *St Michael* and the *St Simon Zelotes*(?), to be painted in an intermediate technique of tempera mixed with oil.

Thus the scientists have proved what already seemed discernible to the eye, that Piero came to the use of the full oil medium gradually. We shall not ever know whether he finally adopted it with the help of the practitioner who came from Ghent to Urbino or whether, as seems much more likely, his absorption in painting the ruler *Portraits* and their *Triumphs* caused him to advise Federico to obtain the services of a Netherlander if he wanted the decoration of his *studiolo* to be done in oils. All that is certain is that in these four pictures he succeeded in uniting the best features of the two great traditions of fifteenth-century Europe.

Later on, there was a complicated picture attributed to Van Eyck in the Palace at Urbino, *A Bath of Women*, but we do not know that it was there already in Federico's time. Certainly there were pictures by Rogier van der Weyden in the Este palaces, where Piero must have seen them. These may even have been painted at Ferrara, though all that is known for certain about Rogier's visit to Italy is that in 1450 he was in Rome. It is not impossible that he and Piero may have become acquainted at Ferrara; but the vignette that has been made from this presumed encounter, of two great artists swapping technical tricks, is scarcely appropriate. The history of Italian painting at this most important juncture has been confused by over-simplification, by the naïf belief that a painter who can discover the technical secret of a Van Eyck thereby becomes capable of reproducing a Van Eyck achievement. The legend of later days that Antonello went to the Netherlands to penetrate Van Eyck's mysteries has long been abandoned; but the fallacy was there already in Vespasiano's almost contemporary and quite credible story that Federico di Montefeltro was sending to Flanders for a painter who knew how to paint on panel in oils when, as we know, Uccello, at least, had left close at hand at Urbino a series of panels painted almost certainly in that medium. Had Vespasiano had some technical knowledge, he would doubtless have written that Federico was looking for an artist who could see and paint like Van Eyck or Van der Weyden.

It is enough to know that Piero must have seen pictures by Rogier almost at the outset of his career. These could not have failed to stimulate his interest in the identification of colour and light and in perspective got by tonal values. Thus memory of Rogier's courtly fastidiousness in idea and in execution is likely to have played some part already in the palace brilliance of the *Allegory with the Flagellation*, painted in tempera though it almost certainly was. For the Netherlandish influence, at least as Piero and, perhaps a little later, the Venetians accepted it, was no mere matter of technique. The fallacy is apt to be extended to include the very content and expression of painting, when Van Eyck becomes the victim of his own incredible success and critics write as if he must actually have had before him everything that he depicted. Evidently he can have had this much less often than Cézanne. If Cézanne had to have recourse to artificial fruits and flowers, how much more would these have been welcome to Van Eyck, whose method of painting in translucent glazes was incomparably more time-consuming! A comparison of the results of these two painters perfectly illustrates the dictum of the philosopher William Whewell that 'there is a mask of theory over the whole face of nature'. We cannot see at all except through the glass of our preconceptions. Van Eyck perhaps had a stronger desire that any other artist to break this glass. His will to see was the most powerful in all the fifteenth century, when in so many parts of Europe artists were throwing off the international style of 'Gothic' to look, in their indigenous ways, at nature.

There is a basic justice in the comparison often made between the 'conceptual' approach of the Italians and the more 'empirical' attitude of the Northerners: but unjust conclusions are apt to be drawn from it. Van Eyck is sometimes represented as almost oblivious of everything but his skill in representing individual forms, as one who can scarcely see the wood for his love of painting every leaf upon the trees. Such a criticism is more fittingly applied to a Gentile da Fabriano. Van Eyck was as much concerned with composition in three dimensions as any other great painter. Italian preconceptions were certainly more ordered. Alberti brought Italy first into the field of aesthetics. That he did so may well have been due to the long tradition of painting on walls and the closer relationship between the painters and the architects. Out of this perhaps came the unique Italian capacity for decorative design, and out of this the system of artificial perspective, with its spectacular and concentrated effects. This Van Eyck did not have; but the fact that there may be half a dozen vanishing points in the scene that he has constructed does not make it any less monumental or a whit less impressive in its human values. His preconceptions were rather those of a humanist-naturalist who sensed the wonder in everything and put the highest value on infinity. This is the summit upon which the two greatest representatives of the two greatest schools of the fifteenth century came together. Both were concerned to make their forms appear utterly tangible, and the oil medium as Van Eyck used it, translucently with paint laid layer upon layer until the forms seemed to glow, each with its particular quality, from within, was the one thing which Piero needed to realise, as Cézanne would have said, the full intensity of his perceptions. Thus more than one happy union are celebrated by the *Triumphs* of Federico and Battista.

1 · The Last Pictures

The Montefeltro *Portraits* and their *Triumphs*, two small, easily portable panels which must nevertheless have occupied Piero for many long months, would naturally have been painted at Sansepolcro, where at least a document attests his presence in the course of 1473. In the following April he received payment for some frescoes in the Madonna Chapel of the Abbey Church (*Badia*) there, his own church; and some four years later he was paid for a *Madonna* by his first known patrons, the Confraternity of the Misericordia, who may also have commissioned of him in the meantime another picture, recorded by the payment made to his brother Marco in 1462 (see p. 51). The *Madonna* was painted on a wall connecting the Misericordia hospital with the church. We do not know even the subject of the Badia paintings, and there is no trace or description of any of these works. These records* are valuable now only in proving the constancy of Piero towards his small home town. Vasari, who states that the frescoes at Arezzo had brought Piero fame and large rewards – they must indeed have opened for him the way to Rome and Urbino – goes on to say that he was able to leave a considerable property, consisting partly of some houses which he had built for himself, though these were burned during the troubles of 1536.

In one house, perhaps the one in which he lived himself, he had painted in fresco the *Hercules* of which the remains are now in the Isabella Stewart Gardner Museum at Boston, Mass. The lower part of this composition, from the middle of the hero's shins, was cut away at some time to make an opening in the wall and there is virtually nothing left of the painted architrave in which Piero set his figure. Within its once generous outlines there is still to be dimly seen the corner of a hall with grey walls and purple timber roof, the corbels carved and the deep red beams painted with classical ornament in grey. The dull richness of these colours has somehow survived, while the light and shade are gone which once must have shown everything in space. Yet the worn figure still retains a broad, magnificent strength. There is a mellow assurance in the draughtsmanship which would seem to justify placing the *Hercules* within this decade of the painter's life, or even later, when he may have had more leisure.

That this is the only picture by Piero, either extant or recorded, which is purely classical in subject is a matter of mainly iconographical interest. From that early moment when he painted *The Baptism* at Sansepolcro he had been, in any but the narrow sense, the most classical of all painters: much too classical to be tempted to borrow romance from Roman ruins or remains, or to incorporate any antique motif not strictly functional in his design. Even in the *Triumphs*, with their theme borrowed from Antiquity, there is no nostalgic tribute paid to Rome. The triumphal cars are field-waggons of the day stripped to the bare essentials of chassis,

---

* The records in this chapter are all given by Longhi, *op. cit.*, pp. 105–7, and De' Vecchi *op. cit.*, p. 84. The necessary references are given in full by Longhi.

wheels and brakes, and that broken column carried in the front of Federico's waggon had long been the attribute of Fortitude, a personification invented by the scholastics of the Middle Ages.

This fundamental classicism seems to have been appreciated by at least a few of his contemporaries even at a time when borrowings from the Antique were coming more than ever into vogue, if we may judge by two scant but often quoted references in contemporary literature. The earlier of these – the earliest of all literary references to Piero – is in Antonio Filarete's 'Treatise on Architecture', believed to have been written a few years after Piero had painted his frescoes in Rome. Here Piero is included on the short list of painters worthy to adorn an ideal building in Milan; and it was Filarete who brought the ideas of Brunelleschi to Milan from Florence. While he had seen and appreciated Piero's frescoes in Rome, Giovanni Santi on the other hand, writing some twenty years later in Urbino, had not necessarily seen any picture by Piero on a large scale. At the moment of writing he was evidently dazed by the brilliance of Mantegna, whose work on walls and panels for the last twenty years and more was largely concentrated at Mantua. In his history of Federico di Montefeltro, written in twenty-four thousand rhyming lines, Santi describes, perhaps out of his imagination, one of the Duke's last pleasures, the sight of Mantegna's pictures at the Mantuan court. In a panegyric upon these and upon Mantegna's absolute supremacy among artists he inserts for comparison a long list of all the others whose names he can remember, and among them

> Masaccio e l'Andrein, Paolo Occelli
> Antonio e Pier sí gran dissegnatori,
> Piero di Borgo antico più di quelli

Santi's choice of words is not often brilliantly apt, and the reaction of Dennistoun, virtually the discoverer of this epic and its translator into English, may be the correct one. He evidently thought that Santi was merely in need of a rhyme for *Occelli* (Uccello) and so filled in with the information that Piero was older than the Pollaiuolo brothers, Antonio and Piero.* But the word *antico* was already in use for neo-classical, and it was not to be long before the Mantuan sculptor Bonacolsi, whose bronzes were inspired by Mantegna's neo-classicism, was christened *Antico*. One is tempted to follow Longhi and, a little against reason in view of the context, believe that Raphael's father, as Santi now was, may have had a flash of insight into the uniquely classical quality of Piero's work.

To retrace our steps to 1478, it is likely to have been in the middle or later part of that year that Piero returned once more to Urbino to take the likeness of the little prince Guidobaldo. The interval had been for central Italy one of almost uninterrupted peace, and the Duke had thus been able to devote nearly all his time to his duchy, tempering the life of absolute ruler with patronage of literature and the arts, himself intent as ever upon 'learning some new thing every day'. He had one great anxiety, the delicate health of his only legitimate son; and the question of the succession, which would normally have been worrying enough in those times of insecurity, seems to have been much upon his mind. In the portrait of father and son which Justus painted, possibly for the centre of the *studiolo* and now

* James Dennistoun, *Memoirs of the Dukes of Urbino*, 1851, volume II, pp. 456–60; he translates all the relevant part of Santi's poem.

restored to Urbino, the Duke is seated reading a great book in full armour, wearing the collar of the Neapolitan Order of the Ermine and the English Garter sent him by Henry VII; but it is poor little Guidobaldo at the age of three or four, standing at his knee in robes of state, who is holding the heavy gold sceptre. In a wider group of two or three years later, which belongs to the Queen of England, the young prince stands to attention in the same position, and no less heavily attired, while the Duke and his intimates sit listening to a lecture from a professor who has been tentatively identified as the astrologer and mathematician Paul of Middleburg, Maestro Paulo, who was later to be Guidobaldo's physician. This panel unfortunately has been indifferently restored over much damage, and it is difficult to say who painted it.

Now the Duke had to leave Urbino to take command of the combined forces of the Papacy and Naples in a protracted and unwilling campaign against Lorenzo de' Medici and Florence. He did not return until late in 1480, and then much aged from the consequences of a bad fall, from which he never fully recovered. The little picture in the Thyssen-Bornemisza collection at Lugano-Castagnola which almost certainly is a *Portrait of Guidobaldo di Montefeltro* shows the boy at an age 67 between six and eight. It is likely therefore to have been painted for his father either in the middle of 1478, just before he set out on this campaign, or during the succeeding months, so that it might be sent after and kept with him in the field. This would account for its very small size and perhaps for its simplicity. There is no landscape here, nor any exaltation: only a jet background for the ivory profile and the golden helmet of silky hair, the tunic of brilliant gold and scarlet damask glimpsed at the neck, the coat of stiff crimson velvet with sleeves embroidered in gold. Simple; but princely enough to gladden any ducal father's heart. Here is a childlike freshness very different from the dazed fatigue of the less inspired portrait-groups. Skin could not be clearer, or hair more fine; cloth could not have a better hang or damask show more clearly the crispness of its gold thread; but the future Duke shows no more consciousness of his fine appearance than does the painter of his skill in rendering it. Perfect manners distinguish both, and the quality of heir apparent to a great and civilised tradition was never stated with greater economy and precision. When I first attributed the little picture to Piero della Francesca in 1964,* I credited the identification of the sitter as Guidobaldo to Federico Zeri. He has since asked me to dissociate him from this idea, and Pierluigi de' Vecchi also rejects this identification of the sitter, while apparently himself accepting the attribution.† The picture came from Urbino as a portrait of the young Raphael by his father. It was bought in 1838 by James Dennistoun, author of the three-volume *Memoirs of the Dukes of Urbino*, 1851, which is still the great authority for the history of Federico and his son.

In 1480 Piero was elected for two years Head of his Guild of St Bartholomew at Sansepolcro. These years, in which there is no other record of him, may well have seen upon his easel *The Nativity* now in the National Gallery. This seems to have been painted for his own devotional purposes, for it has come down to us, like the *Hercules*, through the sons of his brother Marco, to whom he devised half 54 of his estate. It is sometimes described as unfinished. If this were so, it would seem

* *Some Italian Renaissance Pictures in the Thyssen-Bornemisza Collection*, 1964, pp. 17–18.
† De' Vecchi, *op. cit.*, p. 107.

to support the view that the picture was painted for himself or a relative; for, had it been commissioned, the commissioning body could have had it finished without great difficulty, for instance by Piero's disciple Lorentino, even if by now he had long been working on his own in his native Arezzo. But in fact, when the picture was cleaned more than twenty years ago, it became clear that it had been damaged all over in the past too severely to leave any evidence that it had been left un-finished.

The evenings of these days Piero may have devoted to his mathematical studies. At least it can have been no later than this that he finished the Italian version, now in the Parma Library, of his *De Prospectiva Pingendi*, illustrated with drawings and diagrams made and annotated with infinite patience by himself; for it seems to have been during the lifetime of Duke Federico that the Latin version which is now in the Ambrosiana Library, Milan, was presented by the painter to the Library at Urbino. It was translated for him by a fellow-citizen of Sansepolcro, but Piero himself must have done the drawings and diagrams all over again.

In the Spring of 1482 the Duke left Urbino for what proved to be the last time, and was met by Lorenzo de' Medici, now his ally in the cause of saving Ferrara from the ambitions of Pope Sixtus IV, at Sansepolcro. Piero, however, was no longer there. On 22 April he had rented a house and garden from the widow of a certain Ganimede Borelli at Rimini. There is no further record of him either at Rimini or at Sansepolcro for more than five years. Perhaps he was mostly at Urbino. In that September the great Duke was carried mortally ill from the field to Ferrara, where he died in the presence of his elder son Antonio, whom he had had legitimised. He consigned his Duchy to Guidobaldo, now ten years old, and Guidobaldo to Ottaviano Ubaldini, his own nephew, who had long been his confidant. Characteristically, he wished to be buried in the little Gothic church of S. Donato, outside the Urbino walls, and his body was brought back and there interred. But it was not long before the two cousins, who wished to make the city even finer in his memory, decided to erect beside S. Donato a new church to be dedicated to S. Bernardino. As architect they evidently employed the Sienese artist Francesco di Giorgio Martini, who after an interval of a few years had succeeded to Laurana's post at Urbino. Francesco was a sculptor and quite a prolific painter, though on a small scale. It must have been hard to believe, when he painted, for instance, the sweet and gentle little *St Dorothy and the Infant Christ* in the London National Gallery, that he was to become a master of the third dimension and the outstanding military engineer of his day. He completed the palace at Urbino with rich and varied ornamentation and gave an entirely new shape to the adjoining cathedral. His cathedral was destroyed by an earthquake in the eighteenth century, which did much other damage.

Owing to its mountain site Urbino has for the most part, however, escaped industrialisation, to become a university town; and it is among cypress, vines and olives that S. Bernardino still presents its elegantly varied mass to the city across a green cleft in the hills. The choir of the church seems to have been extended later, and this has taken away from the compact perfection of its original form, that of a short cross with rounded head and arms radiating from a tall dome. Not large as a church, it is a grandiose mausoleum, with its height and shapeliness and its utter simplicity. There is nothing in the white nave but two great sarcophagi in polished black marble against the walls, one containing the remains of Federico, the other those of Guidobaldo and his Duchess Elisabetta. On the high altar under the cupola used to stand Piero's last picture, the great altarpiece, *The Virgin and Child with Saints and Angels*, now in the Brera Gallery at Milan.

III-IV

So, had this picture been commissioned a century and a half later of another but more widely famous classicist, we might be looking at the black slippers of the great Generalissimo dangling in space while air-borne Angels lean from billowing clouds to speed his ascension to glory beside the Virgin. But apotheosis, even of 'the light of Italy', was far from the ethos of a Montefeltro. Nor was the allegory of a Piero della Francesca ever prised away from foundations firmly set in the earth. In S. Bernardino the great commander, his last campaign over, is simply come to lay down his baton, with his steel gauntlets and helmet, at the feet of the Madonna. While the Child sleeps on unconscious across her lap, the four Angels and the six Saints attending her are spellbound by the event. Federico had longed for a solemn painter, and Piero has depicted this, his solemn hour as a moment of revelation held in suspense for eternity. If before *The Nativity* one can hear the first of Christmas hymns, before this altarpiece one can feel the silence of a great ending. While the hushed Saints, as they hold their breath, can each look only into his own mind, the whole scene, so tangible and yet so remote, seems to look at us, enjoining us to share their awe. This is surely the most profound representation of silence ever painted in Europe.

To compare it with the only picture by Piero which is comparable as a Madonna composition, the little Clark altarpiece at Williamstown, is to see how the continuous study of nature may continuously enrich design. That picture seemed already characteristic of the great artist in its grave monumentality, the beauty of its colour and its light. To look back at it over some forty years of Piero's painting is to find it cramped and clumsy, the figures less alive and yet more restless, almost noisy by comparison with S. Bernardino and his companions. Each of these is intensely live and individual, and yet all are absolutely still, their pulsating lives suspended, an achievement of infinite subtlety in the description of form. It was space that we found lacking at Williamstown; and space is the great essential, a medium for the expression of silence, the prerequisite for the convincing existence of form. This eternal group is contained and united in a space which we accept as more valid than the actual space in which we are standing to regard it, because of the measured beauty of the dimensions and the rich, translucent colour of the atmosphere which they enclose. Piero's space is warmly human, embracing us too, establishing frontiers for the imagination, even while it stimulates.

The scene is the ultimate development of Masaccio's frescoed recess with *The Trinity* in Florence, which with all its dread power and austere simplicity, may by comparison seem artificial, restless, thin in atmosphere. Piero's composition is of the simplest. There is no grandiose throne to elevate the Madonna above the rest. He has retained the absolute symmetry of the earlier Renaissance, knowing that nothing can be more impressive than a figure placed exactly in the centre, on a strongly marked axis, with all the lines of the perspective converging more or less upon the Virgin's head. The architecture, its formality enlivened by the complex, idealised shape of the great scallop valve projecting from the hollowed quarter-sphere of the apse, participates fully with the richness of its surface and its colour in the illusion of space and coloured light which it encloses. From the centre of the half-shell hangs that perfection in the round, the ostrich egg shell still beloved of Orthodox Greek churches, symbol of the creation and of the four elements. It is used by the painter not only to define more exactly the depth of the apse and the angle of our vision but, above all, as a microcosm of the whole scene. The sunlight flooding from an invisible window high on the left lights a point on its surface with full brilliance. This declines with exquisite gradations into shadow, until that in turn meets and is blended again into the softest light of all, reflected on the other side from the marble of the walls. It is in this way that every figure below is colour-illuminated, the degree of direct and of reflected light varied in intensity not only by the local colour or even by the juxtaposition of other colours but according to its position in the luminous space.

Alas, the whole effect is now sadly distorted, although most of the paint is in excellent condition except for losses along horizontal lines where the nine planks of which the panel is composed have parted – the eyes of the Virgin and of several of the Saints are damaged in this way. With Piero's pictures in general we are fortunate in that, though most are more worn than this, nearly all have been cleaned of recent years, and some have even been effectively restored. In their case freedom from darkened and semi-opaque varnishes and other surface accretions is more than usually important because these obscure altogether the subtlety of his colours and the impression of cool light resulting from their harmony. It is the true light of the clear, blue Italian sky in which he finally achieved the exquisite definition of his forms. Even when he has used rose or crimson, these are clearly lit by cool light, infiltrating the equally pure but intenser colour of the shadows. These facts have been recognised more or less in the cleaning of the majority of Piero's pictures, and it is not difficult with the Urbino *Portraits* and *Triumphs* to make allowance for the yellowed varnish. We are less fortunate over his last and greatest picture. The S. Bernardino altarpiece was cleaned to a certain extent some years ago, and patches of very dark old varnish have been left here and there which may suggest that the remainder of the picture is now as Piero painted it. This is far from the case. There is now no white to 'give gladness' to the colours, no cool tone; and the translucency of the most delicate passages, such as the crystal cross held by St Francis before the wound in his side, the jewels of the Virgin and the Angels, is become almost opaque under the remains of brown varnish. The 'cleaning' was done, alas, by one of those practitioners who dislike cool tones or pure colour and consider that old pictures, like old furniture, should wear a warm 'patina' of old varnish, whatever were the intentions of the artist. This great picture therefore does not have by any means its full effect; its sparkle can be discovered only by close examination, by waiting until the eye has adjusted itself with the aid of reason to a surface which has been deliberately part-obscured by a semi-opaque mélange of old varnish and new.

Slowly, as the visibility improves with our patience and willpower, we are able to comprehend this greatest synthesis of man and nature, compounded of the fifteenth century's power to see and the philosophy of the early humanists. Like those of *The Nativity*, the Angels are solid creatures with all their weight on the ground; but, unlike them, they have wings. A band trained in the duty of waiting on the Virgin, they are in full dress, the uniformity of their ash-blond hair and

Details from *The Flagellation*: xxxi, left-hand half; xxxii, head of figure at right centre; xxxiii, head of figure at far right. Panel 59 × 81.5 cms. Galleria Nazionale delle Marche, Urbino

I

XXXIV

passive stance a foil to the variety of their luxurious dress and ornament. These are painted with so light a brush, with such an aptness of its every touch that it seems to be the agent of the sun itself, searching with unerring skill and perfect taste for the detail which will play the tenderest and most telling part in the swelling harmony of the whole. There is not a touch of bravura, each stroke is the result of patient, constructive research into the beauties which lie in nature awaiting revelation. The technique of the Netherlandish painters is quite transcended, and painting attains to the condition of the finest music, supremely enjoyable in the abstract for the quality and the subtle succession of its notes, even while the harmonies that they construct are penetrating our souls. Only a total harmony of all the elements in nature could contain so tranquilly individualities so powerful as we discover in the Saints: John Baptist, Bernardino, Jerome, Francis, Peter Martyr, John Evangelist(?). I can think of no rendering of a human being more flattering to humanity, more soothing to the self-questioning anguish of its soul, than this St Francis. Nor were tenderness and strength ever better combined than in the drawing of his head and hands and habit

A mutilation which is ultimately more serious because it is permanent is the reduction of the panel all round. All the edges are said to be cut; but there is no information concerning the extent. One would think that there was once more space at least at the foot, to have allowed more room to Federico and have set the Virgin's throne further in, and perhaps at the top, where the plane of the architecture above the alcove is now in danger of becoming confused with the plane of the picture surface, an impression which Piero was careful to avoid already in the Williamstown altarpiece. Can the picture have been considerably taller when it was completed?

This was most probably the first and the last occasion in Piero's career when the altarpiece and the church which was to contain it were conceived at the same time. The altarpiece is planned to suggest the interior of a little temple, a life-size casket completely encrusted with carved ornament or coloured marble and open at one end, to be contained within a much larger building of which it is the principal ornament. It could have stood only upon the high altar, so that the axial line of the nave should lead straight to the figure of the Madonna and continue at right angles through her enthroned figure into the centre of the vault behind, above her head. The cornices which run into the picture plane at either side show that the building represented is conceived as having four symmetrical arches, through one of which we are privileged to see. Since the top of the picture is cut, the question has to be asked: how far was the illusion originally carried with the aid of the frame which has disappeared? Were the lines of these cornices at the sides carried on into the frame, as they were with Giovanni Bellini's huge altarpiece from S. Giobbe in Venice? In Bellini's painting, however, this is made possible by a much shallower building and Saints who stand in the very foreground, at the picture plane. With the S. Bernardino altarpiece such a supposition means that the picture would originally have been higher by a great deal. C. L. Ragghianti* has gone boldly to the full extreme, supposing that the pilasters which should terminate in these cornices were originally shown within the picture itself, together with the whole height of the arch which springs from them and more. This fulfils

* See De' Vecchi, op. cit., pp. 106–7.

XXXIV St Julian (?), fresco 130 × 105 cms. Palazzo Comunale, Sansepolcro

his theory of a golden section on which he thinks the whole composition must have been based, and it makes the egg the mathematical centre of it all. In such a composition, however, the figures become dwarfed by the architecture to a degree which seems incompatible with the humanism of Piero, to whom it would surely have seemed more desirable that the composition should centre, as it does now, very nearly, on the Virgin's head. This it does not do even if the more modest supposition is made that both picture and frame had an arched top and the frame had pilasters supporting cornices which are continued in the picture. Neither of these drastic suppositions seems convincing. The proportions of the picture as it is now seem satisfactory for what Piero wished to express, and there is no reason to suppose that he ever wished to carry the architectural illusion to its logical extreme. It is preferable to think of this altarpiece as no less human than *The Nativity*; indeed as its indoor equivalent, its formal complement on the grander scale of life.

Once more an apocryphal legend, such as attaches itself locally to every conspicuous Italian picture, has perpetuated itself in the views of even serious modern critics. According to this one the altarpiece is a memorial to the Countess Battista, who is represented here as the Virgin, with the infant Guidobaldo (enjoying a physique very different from his own) on her lap. This would date the picture about 1472. Duke Federico, it is true, looks little older than he does in the Uffizi profile, which was probably painted about then, and younger, if anything, than in his portrait with the young Guidobaldo painted by Justus about 1475–6. But why should he not if he was dead? In fact his head is painted in a way quite different from that in which the rest of the altarpiece is painted. While the other heads are built up in Piero's normal way, from below or within, by underpainting, the Duke's head is painted virtually *alla prima*, on the surface, as if copied from another portrait. Indeed, it varies very little from the profile in the Uffizi Gallery except in the angle of the head and the distribution of the light. Federico's hands are painted by another artist: perhaps Justus, perhaps his former pupil and assistant Berruguete. The church of S. Bernardino was consecrated in 1491;[*] and the argument that S. Bernardino happened by good fortune to be included in a picture painted beforehand for some other church unknown and transferred later is discountenanced by the presence in the altarpiece of Piero's fellow-citizen and mathematical disciple Luca Pacioli, whose head and shoulders appear discreetly enough behind St Francis in the character of St Peter Martyr. Pacioli was born about 1445–50, and he was certainly not still in his twenties when Piero painted this likeness. Indeed this identification rests upon a portrait at Capodimonte, Naples, by an unidentified artist who inscribed it IACO BAR *Vigen /nis* 1495 *p.*, and incidentally made Pacioli look very little older in 1495 than he appears in Piero's altarpiece. There is no doubt that Pacioli is the subject of the Capodimonte picture, for the closed book on the table behind which he stands, like a conjuror, is inscribed LI.R.LUC.BUR (presumably for LIBER REVERENDI LUCAE BURGENSIS), and the book is weighted by a bronze model of a dodecahedron. In the air is suspended another in crystal of an icosahexahedron, a volume of twenty-six facets, below which the mathematician is demonstrating on a slate how to inscribe an equilateral triangle within a circle. The pupil or patron behind him is richly

* Pasquate Rotondi, *Guida del Palazzo Ducale di Urbino*, 1948, p. 177.

attired; but, although his age appears suitable, it is difficult to accept the suggestion that the person consigned to this secondary place is none other than Duke Guidobaldo.

Vasari launches into his biography of Piero with a violent denunciation of Pacioli for defrauding the painter of the honour due to him for his mathematical works. He did indeed incorporate the whole of Piero's treatise *De Quinque Corporibus Regolaribus* into his own *De Divina Proportione* without acknowledgement. In the preface to an earlier book, the *Summa de arithmetica, geometria, proportione e proportionalitate*, published in Venice two years after Piero's death, Pacioli, it is true, called Piero the prince of contemporary painting and architecture; but this, if it shows that he had some conscience, can hardly be called making amends. Pacioli was not the first or the last to pretend that the perfection of a work of art depended upon the use of rule and compass, and so upon the mathematical wizards, of whom he was the most conspicuous in his day. The inclusion of his portrait in the S. Bernardino altarpiece suggests that Piero was his friend, perhaps his teacher; and it is not impossible that Pacioli gave Piero some assistance in producing his treatise on the five basic volumes and was able to remain in possession of his original manuscript in Italian. All that exists today is the Latin *De Quinque Corporibus Regolaribus*, now in the Vatican Library, with figures drawn by Piero himself and a lengthy dedication to Duke Guidobaldo in his own hand. In this he describes the new treatise as written in the extremity of his span of life, 'in order to save his brain from becoming torpid through inactivity'.

Thus its production must have coincided, more or less, with the painting of the S. Bernardino altarpiece. It may be presumed that this was in its place when the church was dedicated in 1491. The painting is by Piero at his best throughout, except for the Duke's hands, which were painted plainly not by an assistant of his but in an entirely different style.* Was this the moment, when all but these hands was completed, that Piero was stricken with blindness? Vasari represents the calamity as having happened suddenly but much earlier in his life, and the tradition of long years of blindness lingers. This is disproved, and not only by the history of the altarpiece. On 5 July 1487, at Sansepolcro, Piero had written his will, now preserved in the State Archives at Florence, in his own hand, stating that he was 'sound in mind, in intellect and in body'. It is surely a model to the lawyers:

I wish to be buried in the *badia*, in our grave. I bequeath to the *badia* treasury ten lire, and to the *corpus christi* ten lire, and to the *madonna of the badia* ten lire and ten lire to the *madonna de lareghia* and of the rest of my estate I leave one half to my brother antonio and if antonio should die before me to his male children and the other half to the heirs of marco that is *francesco*, *bastiano* and *girolamo* and if one of them dies it goes from one to the other.

If the altarpiece indeed went on exhibition in 1491, Piero's failure to finish it himself provides strong evidence that his wonderful eyesight had predeceased his other faculties, for he lived until the autumn of 1492. Chance has preserved corroborative evidence in a sad little entry in a commonplace book of the next century – the only record that we have concerning Piero's person. In 1556 Berto degli

---

* Some, including the author, think the hands are by Justus, others by Berruguete. Unfortunately there are no original documents concerning the work of either in the palace at Urbino.

Alberti wrote down what had been told him by a lantern-maker, Marco di Longaro:

'The said Marco, when he was little, used to lead about by the hand Master *Piero dila Francesca*, excellent painter, who was blind; so he told me.'

In the Palazzo Pretorio, now the Museo Civico, at Borgo Sansepolcro, in the room which still houses his glowing *Resurrection*, one may read the record of Piero's death, made by the Guild of St Bartholomew of which he had been two years Prior:

'*M. Pietro di Benedetto de' Franceschi* famous painter on 12 October 1492; buried in the Badia.'

He may have been eighty years old.

Catalogue

The order is, approximately, according to the author's opinions on chronology, and, with some exceptions, that in which the pictures are mentioned in the body of the text. The page and plate references are given at the foot of each entry.

Where the work consists of more than one painting the order is always from left to right. The measurements, in metres, are approximate, and refer to the painted surface. The medium is stated only if this has been established by analysis. The date given is inscribed.

POLYPTYCH: THE MADONNA DELLA MISERICORDIA

Wood, with 3 panels originally on the lower (main) tier, 5 originally on the upper (the paintings forming the *predella* and pilasters are not by Piero)

Main Tier

SS. SEBASTIAN AND JOHN BAPTIST, 1.08 × 0.90
THE MADONNA DELLA MISERICORDIA, 1.34 × 0.91
SS. JOHN EVANGELIST AND BERNARDINO, 1.08 × 0.90

Upper Tier

ST BENEDICT, 0.54 × 0.21
THE ANNOUNCING ARCHANGEL, 0.55 × 0.205
THE CRUCIFIXION, 0.81 × 0.525
THE ANNUNCIATE VIRGIN, 0.54 × 0.21
ST FRANCIS, 0.545 × 0.21
Borgo Sansepolcro, Pinacoteca Comunale
See pp. 47–52 and v–xiv and 23

THE MADONNA AND CHILD WITH FOUR ANGELS

Wood, 1.06 × 0.78. Williamstown, Mass., Sterling and Francine Clark Art Institute
See pp. 61–2 and 50–3

SIGISMONDO MALATESTA KNEELING TO ST SIGISMUND .1451

Plaster, 2.57 × 3.45. Rimini, Duomo
See pp. 63–7 and 24

GEROLAMO AMADI KNEELING TO ST JEROME

Wood, 0.49 × 0.42. Venice, Gallerie dell'Accademia
See pp. 67–8 and 21

THE CRUCIFIXION

Wood, 0.355 × 0.405. New York, Frick Collection
See p. 69 and 63

THE BAPTISM OF CHRIST
Tempera on wood, 1.67 × 1.16. London, National Gallery
See pp. 69–72 and 22

ST JULIAN (?): a fragment
Plaster, 1.30 × 1.05. Borgo Sansepolcro, Pinacoteca Comunale
See p. 120 and XXXIV and 26

DECORATION OF A CHAPEL: THE LEGEND
OF THE HOLY CROSS, AND OTHER SUBJECTS
Plaster, on 3 walls with scenes in 3 tiers on each. On the 2 side walls the top tiers measure about 3.90 × 7.45, the centre tier about 3.35 × 7.45, the lowest tier about 3.20 × 7.45. On the narrower window wall the two upper rectangular scenes measure each about 3.55 × 1.90, the two lower about 3.30 × 1.90.
Arezzo, S. Francesco, Principal Chapel
See pp. 79–91 and XV–XXV and 28–44

ST LUKE
Plaster. The figure is not less than life size.
Rome, Sta Maria Maggiore, porch (former Cappella dei SS. Michele e Pietro)
See p. 111 and 27

THE MADONNA DEL PARTO
Plaster (surface removed from the wall to canvas), 2.60 × 2.03
Cemetery outside Monterchi, near Sansepolcro, Mortuary Chapel
See p. 112 and 46–7

THE RESURRECTION
Plaster, 2.25 × 2.00. Borgo Sansepolcro, Pinacoteca Comunale
See pp. 112–3 and XXVI–XXVIII and 49

ST LOUIS: a fragment
Plaster, 1.23 × 0.90. Borgo Sansepolcro, Pinacoteca Comunale
See p. 113 and 48

AN ALLEGORY WITH THE FLAGELLATION
Wood, 0.59 × 0.815. Urbino, National Gallery for the Marches
See pp. 115–7 and XXXI–XXXIII and 25

THE MADONNA AND CHILD WITH TWO ANGELS
Wood, 0.61 × 0.535. Urbino, National Gallery for the Marches
See pp. 117–8 and XXIX–XXX and 66

POLYPTYCH: THE MADONNA AND CHILD ENTHRONED,
WITH SAINTS
Wood, with 3 panels on the main tier, a single panel with *The Annunciation* above and 3 *predella* panels below. Between the *predella* and the main tier have been inserted 2 painted roundels, each with a *Saint*, which originally were probably between the main tier and *The Annunciation*.

SS. ANTHONY OF PADUA AND JOHN BAPTIST, 1.24 × 0.62
THE MADONNA AND CHILD ENTHRONED, 1.41 × 0.65
SS. FRANCIS AND ELIZABETH, 1.24 × 0.64

Upper Tier

THE ANNUNCIATION, 1.22 × 1.94

Predella

ST ANTHONY RESUSCITATES A DEAD BABY, 0.365 × 0.49
THE STIGMATISATION OF ST FRANCIS, 0.365 × 0.515
ST ELIZABETH SAVES A CHILD FROM A WELL, 0.365 × 0.45

Also

ST CLARE (?), 0.21 × 0.38 (including decoration)
ST AGATHA, 0.21 × 0.38 (including decoration)
Perugia, National Gallery for Umbria
See pp. 125–34 and 64

ST AUGUSTINE
Wood, 1.33 × 0.60
Lisbon, Museu de Arte Antiga
See p. 124 and 59
This and the 3 pictures following were parts of an altarpiece of which the centre is missing. The 3 smaller pictures following after *St Nicholas of Tolentino* probably also belonged to it. Possibly also *The Crucixion* of the Frick Collection.

ST MICHAEL
Tempera and oil on wood, 1.33 × 0.595. London, National Gallery
See p. 122 and 60

ST SIMON ZELOTES (?)
Tempera and oil on wood, 1.315 × 0.578. New York, Frick Collection
See p. 123 and 61

ST NICHOLAS OF TOLENTINO
Wood, 1.33 × 0.60. Milan, Poldi-Pezzoli Museum
See pp. 124–5 and 62

ST MONICA
Wood, 0.39 × 0.28. New York, Frick Collection
See p. 121

AN AUGUSTINIAN SAINT
Wood, p.39 × 0.26. New York, Frick Collection
See p. 121

ST APOLLONIA
Wood, 0.41 × 0.28. Washington, D.C., National Gallery
See p. 121

ST MARY MAGDALEN
Plaster, 1.90 high. Arezzo, Duomo
See p. 119 and 45

DIPTYCH: PORTRAITS OF COUNT FEDERICO DI MONTE-
FELTRO AND THE COUNTESS BATTISTA, WITH THEIR
TRIUMPHS
Wood, two panels, each 0.47 × 0.33, painted on both sides

Obverse

BATTISTA SFORZA, COUNTESS OF URBINO
FEDERICO DI MONTEFELTRO, COUNT OF URBINO

Reverse

THE TRIUMPH OF COUNTESS BATTISTA
THE TRIUMPH OF COUNT FEDERICO
Urbino, National Gallery for the Marches
See pp. 135–42 and 55–8

HERCULES
Plaster, 1.51 × 1.26. Boston, Mass., Isabella Stewart Gardner Museum
See p. 143 and 54

THE NATIVITY
Oil on wood, 1.245 × 1.23. London, National Gallery
See pp. 11–8 and I–II and 65

PORTRAIT OF GUIDOBALDO DI MONTEFELTRO(?)
AS A BOY
Wood, 0.41 × 0.275. Lugano-Castagnola, Thyssen-Bornemisza Collection
See p. 145 and 67

FEDERICO DI MONTEFELTRO, DUKE OF URBINO,
KNEELING BEFORE THE MADONNA AND CHILD,
WITH SAINTS AND ANGELS
Wood, 2.48 × 1.70. Milan, Brera Gallery
See p. 147–54 and III–IV

THE ILLUSTRATIONS

Illustrations 1–19 are for critical comparison
Illustrations 20–6f. are works by Piero della Francesca

1. Alesso Baldovinetti: *The Nativity*, SS Annunziata, Florence

2. Master of San Francesco: *Crucifix*, National Gallery, London

3. Masaccio: *The Trinity with the Virgin and St John and the Donors*, Sta Maria Novella, Florence

4. Masaccio: *The Tribute Money*, Sta Maria del Carmine, Florence

5. (Opposite) Masaccio: *The Crucifixion*, Galleria Nazionale di Capodimonte, Naples

6. Fra Angelico: *The Annunciation*, Museo Diocesano, Cortona

a. Fra Angelico: *The Marriage of the Virgin* and *The Visitation*,
detail of the predella, Museo Diocesano, Cortona

b. Fra Angelico: *The Visitation* and *The Adoration of the Kings* (see 7a)

c. Fra Angelico: *The Presentation in the Temple* and *The Dormition of the Virgin* (see 7a)

8. Fra Angelico: *The Deposition*, S. Marco, Florence

rri Spinelli: *Madonna della Misericordia*, Sta Maria delle Grazie, Arezzo

10a. Paolo Uccello: *The Creation of Adam*, cloister of Sta Maria Novella, Florence

10b. Detail of 10a

(Opposite) Paolo Uccello: figure from *The Flood* (detail of 12b)

Paolo Uccello: *The Flood*, cloister of Sta Maria Novella, Florence

13a. Paolo Uccello: *The Battle of San Romano*, National Gallery, London

13b. Paolo Uccello: *The Battle of San Romano*, Uffizi, Florence

13c. Paolo Uccello: *The Battle of San Romano*, Louvre, Paris

14a. Paolo Uccello: *The Profanation of the Host*, Galleria Nazionale delle Marche, Urbino

14b. See 14a

14c. See 14a

14d. See 14a

15. Andrea del Castagno: *The Last Supper*, Convent of Sta Apollonia, Florence

16. (Opposite) Spinello Aretino: *St Michael*, S. Francesco, Arezzo

17. Justus of Ghent: *The Communion of the Apostles*,
Galleria Nazionale delle Marche, Urbino

18a. Justus of Ghent: *Dante*,
Louvre, Paris

18b. Justus of Ghent: *Cardinal Bessarion*,
Louvre, Paris

19. Domenico Veneziano: *Virgin and Child enthroned, with Four Saints*, Uffizi, Florence

WORKS BY PIERO DELLA FRANCESCA

20. *Madonna and Child*, panel 53 × 41 cms. Contini Bonacossi Collection, Florence. Possibly an immature work by Piero. Longhi and others attribute it to him without question.

21. *Gerolamo Amadi kneeling to St Jerome*, panel 40 × 42 cms.
Galleria dell' Accademia, Venice

22. (Opposite) *The Baptism of Christ*, panel 167 × 116 cms.
National Gallery, London

23. *The Polyptych of the Misericordia,*
panel 273 × 323 cms (overall dimensions). Palazzo Comunale, Sansepolcro

·SANCTVS·SIGISMVNDVS· ·HIERVMVNDVS·PAND

24. *Sigismondo Malatesta kneeling to St Sigismund,*
fresco 257×345 cms, 1451.
Tempio Malatestiano, Rimini

25. *An Allegory,*
with The Flagellation,
panel 59 × 81·5 cms.
Galleria Nazionale
delle Marche, Urbino

26. *St Julian* (?), fresco 130 × 105 cms. Palazzo Comunale, Sansepolcro

27. *St Luke*, fresco. Sta Maria Maggiore, Rome

28. *The Death of Adam*,
fresco 390 × 747 cms.
S. Francesco, Arezzo

29. *The Queen of Sheba Worshipping the Wood of the Cross*
and *The Reception of the Queen of Sheba by King Solomon*, fresco 336×747 cms. S. Francesco, Arezzo

30. *The Queen of Sheba's Prophecy*,
fresco 356 × 190 cms. S. Francesco, Arezzo

31. *The Annunciation*,
fresco 329×193 cms. S. Francesco, Arezzo

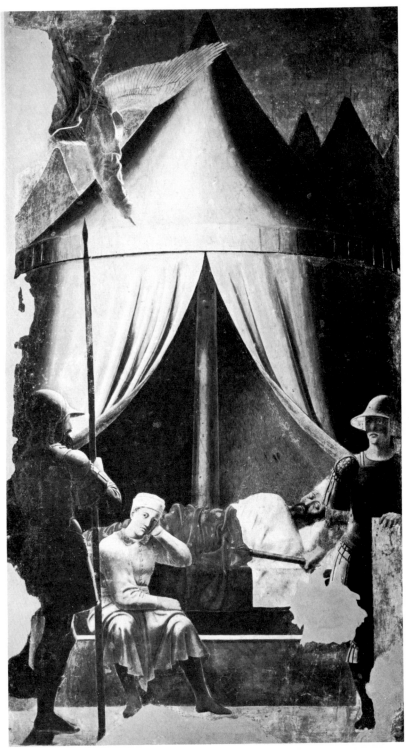

32. *The Dream of Constantine*, fresco 329 × 190 cms. S. Francesco, Arezzo

33. *Judas drawn from the Well*, fresco 356×193 cms. S. Francesco, Arezzo

34. *The Victory of Constantine over Maxentius*, fresco 322 × 764 cms. S. Francesco, Arezzo

35. *The Discovery of the Crosses* and *The Identification of the Holy Cross*, fresco 356 × 747 cms. S. Francesco, Arezzo

36. *The Victory of Heraclius* and *The Execution of Chosroes*, fresco 329 × 747 cms. S. Francesco,

37. *The Return of the Cross to Jerusalem*, fresco 390×747 cms. S. Francesco, Arezzo→

38. (Opposite) *St Augustine* (largely by Bicci di Lorenzo), fresco base 72 cms. S. Francesco, Arezzo

39 and 40. *Angels' Heads* (begun by Bicci di Lorenzo), fresco base 55 cms. S. Francesco, Arezzo

41. (Overleaf left) *A Prophet*, fresco base 193 cms. S. Francesco, Arezzo

42. (Overleaf right) *A Prophet*, fresco base 190 cms. S. Francesco, Arezzo

43. (Opposite) *St Peter Martyr*, fresco base 70 cms. S. Francesco, Arezzo

44. *An Archangel*, fresco base 70 cms. S. Francesco, Arezzo

45. (Opposite) *St Mary Magdalen*, fresco 190 × 180 cms. Arezzo Cathedral

46. *Madonna del Parto*, fresco 260 × 203 cms. Cemetery Chapel, Monterchi, Sansepolcro

47. Detail of 46

48. *St Louis*, fresco 123 × 90 cms, 1460. Palazzo Comunale, Sansepolcro

49. *The Resurrection*, fresco 225 × 200 cms. Palazzo Comunale, Sansepolcro

50. *Madonna and Child with Four Angels*,
panel 106 × 78 cms. Clark Institute, Williamstown, Mass

51. (Opposite) Detail of 50

52. Detail of 50

53. Detail of 50

54. (Opposite) *Hercules*, fresco 151 × 126 cms. Isabella Stewart Gardner Museum, Boston, Mass

55 and 56. *Battista Sforza* and *Federico da Montefeltro*, panel 47 × 33 cms. Uffizi, Florence

CLARVS INSIGNI VEHITVR TRIVMPHO ·
QVEM PAREM SVMMIS DVCIBVS PERHENNIS ·
FAMA VIRTVTVM CELEBRAT DECENTER ·
SCEPTRA TENENTEM

57. *The Triumph of Federico, Duke of Urbino* (see 55 and 56)

QVE MODVM REBVS TENVIT SECVNDIS
CONIVGIS MAGNI DECORATA RERVM
LAVDE GESTARVM VOLITAT PER ORA
CVNCTA VIRORVM

58. *The Triumph of Battista, Duchess of Urbino* (see 55 and 56)

59. *St Augustine*,
panel 133 × 60 cms. Museu de Arte Antiga, Lisbon

60. *St Michael*,
panel 133 × 59·5 cms. National Gallery, London

61. *St Simon Zelotes* (?)

panel 131·5 × 57·8 cms. Frick Collection, New York

62. *St Nicholas of Tolentino*,
panel 133 × 60 cms, Museo Poldi Pezzoli, Milan

63. *The Crucifixion*, panel 35·5 × 40·5 cms. Frick Collection, New York (J. D. Rockefeller Bequest)

64. *The St Anthony Polyptych*, panel 338 × 230 cms (overall dimensions).
Galleria Nazionale dell'Umbria, Perugia

65. (Opposite) Detail from *The Nativity*,
group of figures at right, panel 124·5 × 123 cms. National Gallery, London

66. *The Madonna and Child with Two Angels*,
panel 61 × 53·5 cms. Galleria Nazionale delle Marche, Urbino

67. *Guidobaldo da Montefeltro* (?),
oil on panel 41 × 27·5 cms. Von Thyssen Collection, Lugano

Acknowledgements

The photographs in colour are by Mario Carrieri, except for I and II, which are by John Freeman and reproduced by courtesy of the Trustees, The National Gallery, London.

The photographs in black and white are from; Alinari, 20, 45, 57, 59; Anderson, 25, 28, 30, 31, 33, 34, 35, 36, 41, 42, 66; Alinari-Mansell, 1, 4, 5, 6, 7, 8, 10a, 10b, 11, 12a, 12b, 13b, 13c, 14a, 14b, 14c, 14d, 15, 17, 19, 21, 29; Anderson-Mansell, 3, 9, 16; Brogi, 48, 49, 58, 62; Bullaty-Lomeo, N.Y., 67; Clark Institute, Williamstown, Mass, 50, 51, 52, 53; Frick Collection, N.Y., 61, 63; Giraudon, Paris, 18a, 18b; Isabella Stewart Gardner Museum, Boston, Mass, 54; National Gallery, London, 2, 13a, 22, 60, 65; Soprintendenza alle Gallerie, Uffizi, Florence, 23, 24, 38, 39, 40, 46, 47, 55, 56.

The jacket illustrations are from Scala, Florence.

Index

Entries in italics refer to the black-and-white illustrations, Roman numerals to the colour plates.